PRINCE

of

SAND

By Duval Farrar

For Terry –
All the best,

[signature]

[signature] Duval Java

3.3.18

For Andrew, Wiatt and Leslie.

CHAPTERS

PRINCE of SAND - Chapter One ... Frères Africains / African Brothers

"Prince, please tell us one of your stories." Many have called to me in this way over the years. It is because I have much to tell.

The West African Yoruban people live in the kingdom of Dahomey where we worshiped *Vordun*. They were once my people, *Vordun* once my god.

The year of my birth was 1744. My memories of the bush and of the forest were pleasing and for a number of years I would sleep and dream of these places. The dreams then stopped.

Our small tribe lived better than most. We were brave warriors when needed but smart enough to keep out of Agaja's way whenever possible. Agaja was a powerful ruler demanding loyalty of the largest tribes in Dahomey where no one was free from his reach. I am proud to say that my father, Kalem, was one of our most respected elders. Young hunters often sought his advice. Kalem would tell them,

"Hunt these forests with *Vordun's* blessing. Feed our village well and you will be favored with many wives. Do not try to fool Agaja's men by sending them deeper into the darkness of the forest but share with them the places where you go to kill our meat. Better to give them a meal and watch them leave in peace. We will feast soon enough after they have left us."

My name in our family was Yamar but in the village I was simply known as Prince.

After some time, even my father called me Prince but my mother always called to me as Yamar.

I was now a warrior of our village as my sixteenth birthday had passed. Much was changing in my life and I felt strong. I had done my part in helping track a lion recently hunted by five of our best men. All in the village understood that I was being tested on this hunt. Two nights following the kill we had completed our journey back to the village and there was a great celebration. Our chests and faces were painted with blood from the hunt and dances were performed to honor the lion. Proudly my father offered me one of his younger wives. As was the practice, I bowed to him but did not take her. Instead I offered my mother a token from the hunt and honored her before the village. This pleased my father.

My friends and I planned to hunt the wild pigs that moved along the trails in the bush leading to the river. This was a one-day journey to the northeast of the village. Hunting the surrounding area was a routine part of a boy's life growing up in a Yoruban village. Only when he became older would a boy join his father and other village warriors on safari that was more than one full day from the village. The dangers of a hunt presented by the elements and the prey were real enough but the threat from larger tribes increased the danger considerably. The farther one moved from the village, the greater the chance of being tracked by enemy tribes from the larger region. When danger was present, warriors needed to work together and use the forest to our advantage. You were trained to accept the cover that *Erinles*, spirit of the forest, provided. Six or eight men learned to move as one, swiftly and silently disappearing under the jungle canopy or melting into the bush that covered the plateau. Only by tracking the tracker, by learning to stalk the hunter could one become one with his surroundings. When a warrior trained his son on such a hunt, it was only with the approval of other hunters. All understood that the boy's safety was his father's sole responsibility. Proudly, when challenged, the Yoruban tribesmen were known to move with great speed over a great distance of difficult terrain without speaking or stopping for food or drink. Rather than running away, maneuvers were often made to circle back on an enemy to track them hoping to learn anything one might later use against them. In addition to stamina, our warriors were trained to rely on nerves of steel when danger was present. Men behaved as men under such conditions. Boys grew up quickly.

I felt strong and there would be seven of us tracking the wild pigs known to feed near the river. My father and others reminded me that we were not to travel beyond the falls in the river that was one night away from the village.

"Prince, look carefully across the trail as you position hunters to spear the pigs that pass between you on the trail. Make space between the men so you are not throwing spears at each other from across the trail."

The necessary preparations had been made and we departed early as the sun began to rise in a cloudless sky. The day was fresh, the air clean. Our breath was warm in the morning chill as we settled into a comfortable pace. Seven young men, we ran easily in single file. Moving quietly over the trail, the last person in line would move out from the group, stretch the pace and accelerate past the other six before slowing his pace and taking a turn in front of the line. This rotation from the rear to the lead position repeated itself throughout the morning and pulled our group forward over familiar trails. We were young. We were free, each of us alone with his thoughts as we traveled as one. We were free men on the hunt to help feed our families. We were happy.

Malek, the strongest of our group, teased us as he ran,

"Why are you women breathing so hard?" he asked as he took his turn to run past us to the front of the line.

All of us knew that Malek felt no pain on the trail. Tall, his arms and legs were long. Malek's body was perfect and he could run all day. Soon the dawn would be coming again. We had come within sight of the river at sunset. We rested and ate on a bluff looking north up the river. After a few hours of sleep, we were moving again at a slower pace through the darkness. The seven of us needed to be in position well ahead of the dawn, listening for movement along the trails winding down the slope to the water's edge. Even after a full day at a fast pace, Batou and Mamout, my two closest companions, were eager and focused. Two others in our group, young husbands with children of their own, were a few years older and seemed to be straining to maintain the pace. No worry as I knew we would soon take our places on both sides of the trail to wait in ambush hoping for game to move through our position. Batou, Mamout, Malek and Prince – we were skilled hunters soon to be strapping wild pig to saplings we would cut to carry our meat over the trails returning home. It seemed to me that no other hunting party could have matched our speed and stealth moving into the killing zone. No, you could not convince me otherwise and I almost felt sorry for the pigs that seemed certain to fall into our trap. My body was that of a young man but I was following the instructions from the mind of a child.

"I am Prince and I am a man to be reckoned with, a warrior of the Yoruba!"

But I was a boy, the foolish boy so pleased with himself to be racing over open fields proving his strength and measuring it against that of his playmates. We were young, so very young. Mistakes we made were the foolish errors of children who mean no harm. If only *Ayza*, our protector spirit, had been watching over us on that day, but she had turned her head away as a small moon hung low in the sky.

To the north were the tribes closely tied to the powerful Agaja and loyal to his command. These villages were strong and they were growing. That was a problem. In 1760 in West Africa there were many mouths to feed, too many. The bounty from a successful hunt would be shared within the village subject to rationing the rewards first to Agaja and then among the larger group. While the hunters themselves received a larger share than other men in the village, sharing first with Agaja and then with all others often left even successful hunters with a hungry belly. Three hungry men from one of these northern villages had taken matters into their own hands. The leader among these three, Oland, and the other two had slipped away early the day before. If all went according to plan, they hoped to complete a successful hunt and return to camp within a period of three days. They told their wives to tell anyone who asked that they were scouting for water buffalo and wild pigs to the south in the valley fed by the river. With only three of them gone it was probable that that there would be little or no notice taken. Should their rogue hunt succeed, they would return with more than enough pigs to satisfy the elders while keeping a larger share of the hunt for themselves. Oland decided it would be better to seek forgiveness than to ask for permission. If the hunt failed, they would stand by their story and go about their business as if no hunt had taken place. Oland did not like to go off in this way and possibly be punished by the tribe but he felt it was worth the risk. The hunger made him do these things.

These three men took up their positions. Oland was concealed in the bush on the high side of the trail. The other two men were perched over the trail on limbs of the largest tree on the low side of the trail. Between them they held the edges of a large heavy net.

Oland had instructed them, "Lay one end across this smooth limb. You two hold the other end here. Be sure to pull the net free from the smooth limb before dropping your end. Let the weight of the net help us."

Oland was across the trail facing down the slope toward the river. They were in a kind of funnel with the trail running between the slope on the left and the trees across to the right of the path. Their method relied as much on luck as it did on skill. With only three hunters to put in place, they had to gamble that they would all three be in the right place at the right time. If not, they would return home empty handed to disappointed wives and hungry children. If the net could be dropped over their prey,

Oland would be in position with his spear and heavy club to take down the pack leader and begin beating any followers into submission while his two net handlers dropped from the tree. As a team of three they would then work together to bag their catch. Oland had made sure they were in place a good three hours before the dawn. Total silence was key. If *Damballah-wedo*, the serpent spirit, walked with them today they would silently strike their prey and wrap them in their deadly net. They prayed that there would be activity on the trail below them at dawn. Hopefully by late afternoon they would be on their way home with the bounty from their hunt. If the trails were empty this morning, they would be gone before noon and hurry home without incident. Oland dared to hope that this would prove to be a lucky day.

Further up the trail and higher on the slope I gathered with two my companions. With hand signals I silently directed them into position on the right side of the trail. I joined them as three others on our hunt concealed themselves across from us on the high side of the trail. Our last hunter, Malek, went about twenty yards further down the trail. Should a group of pigs come through, six of us would try to spear them within our gauntlet while Malek would be in place to pick off any target that made it past our trap. Often this last hunter finished off a wounded pig that might otherwise escape into the bush only to be taken by some wild predator or scavenger lurking down near the river. If we were effective with our spears, Malek's job further down the trail would be easy. If startled pigs bolted past us charging down the trail, Malek would be in the path of panicked prey ready to fight their way through any danger. It was now more than two hours before the dawn as we settled in to wait.

For hours we sat in silence. Faint light began to filter into the darkness. Sounds of the bush were amplified and distinct. The sharp snap of a stick being broken further up the trail startled us as dim light was now beginning to define the horizon across the river. The breeze freshened through the trees. The first birds of morning began their calls. Familiar sounds were interrupted when the stick snapped. Straining, we now heard the shuffling of prey moving closer. Definitely there was movement on the trail. There was now just enough light in the sky to help us see what was coming our way. Breaks in the bush concealing the trail allowed us to catch a glimpse of a group of wild pigs making their way down toward the river and directly into our trap. It felt as if everything was moving very slowly. I focused on the two large sows leading what seemed to be about eight animals down the trail. The voice in my head screamed that the banging of my heart was certain to scare the pigs. My palms were damp, my mouth dry. The first sow was moving quickly toward us from my left as steel glinted in the corner of my right eye. Mamout, crouched to my right, had raised up in an instant. His long right arm held his spear high over his shoulder. Perfectly placed, the spear sliced cleanly deep into the sow's right shoulder where it meets the neck and she immediately went to her knees. On my left, Batou had stood, his right thigh flexed. He grunted loudly hurling his spear at the second pig. His effort was off the mark as the blade lodged high on the sow's back. Batou began to run after the wounded animal calling out to Malek that the large pig was racing toward him. Action erupted and our men across the trail joined me in spearing the smaller pigs following in line on the heels of the two sows. Squealing of the pigs was loud in our ears but my mind was already rejoicing at our good fortune. We had successfully laid our trap and wild pigs were falling before us. Mamout and I grabbed our second spears and hurried down the trail to try and help Batou and Malek kill the wounded sow. Across the trail our three men remained in place delivering killing blows to the four smaller pigs we had taken down.

Malek had moved further down the trail shifting to the high side of the path. The bloodied sow raced toward him with Batou's spear bouncing crazily about as it remained lodged in the right side of her back.

I was shouting, "Malek, take her! Take her down!"

Malek's blade plunged into her left shoulder and she was finished. We were smiling in a moment of relative quiet when we first heard the boar. Malek and Batou were standing in the trail at the head of the dead sow facing back up the trail. Mamout and I turned as one when we heard something large crashing through the bush. I first saw him as he stumbled down onto the trail and swerved to his left. This brought him charging directly toward us.

"Fuck", Malek grunted under his breath.

This huge male was by far the biggest pig we had ever seen. Fearful to behold, the tusks were grotesque and eyes red with fury. The monster was on us. We hurled spears as he slammed into Malek goring him in his right groin. The brute force of the boar's charge drove us all yards further down the trail beneath a large tree that stood on the right side of the path. One spear dangled from the boar's belly. Malek was screaming as the beast pinned him to the ground. It seemed that hot blood was being sprayed like a waterfall. And in this moment of horror my life was over and my life began, forever changed.

Malek's arms flailed at the back of the boar's neck in an effort to cushion the blow but it made no difference. The animal's shoulders bulged, all muscle and hard like iron. His hooves were steel hammers tearing up turf, roots and rocks. Anything in his path was ripped away. His snout remained low to the ground. And then, as he felt Malek's weight on his shoulders, he braced his front legs and simply raised his granite neck with such force that instantly the tusks sliced through Malek's thighs. Blood, Malek's blood, was pouring down the pig's snout and neck. Human flesh was laid open and the brutal sound of bone shattering made me vomit. The boar's hot breath was foul. I tried to raise my head as the weight of a heavy net fell on my shoulders and neck.

I could not understand and was in total disbelief. A *NET?* Raging fear came over me as the net fell on us. From where and how and why and who and now, as three of us were trying to kill the boar that was destroying Malek, we were bound and tangled together in netting that had been dropped on us. From somewhere I saw a spear slicing into the huge boar as the back of my neck was struck and suddenly exploded in pain. I lost consciousness from the blow and mercifully could recall no more of our capture.

Water was thrown in my face as I was being pushed up into a sitting position. My hands were tied, my ankles bound and something strange was around my neck. Pure pain ran from the top of my head into my neck and shoulders. What I could see and hear crushed me. Mamout and Batou were sitting on my left bound in the same manner. As I leaned forward to look to my right I realized that the collar around my neck was connected by chain to the collar on Mamout. Two of the other men from our group were chained together and sitting to my right. Malek and Ganja, the last two of our group, were nowhere to be seen. The huge boar, once the target of our hunt, lay dead in the middle of the blood drenched trail. I had never seen the three men who were now moving among us and ordering us to sit up. Suddenly it was as clear to me as the sun rising above. We, seven strong young hunters, had actually been their prey. These men did not hunt for meat but to take prisoners from the bush. Silent tears burned my cheeks. I was afraid and I was deeply shamed.

My first thought in captivity was to ask Mamout where Malek and Ganja had gone. Before I could finish the question I was brutally struck across the face with a handful of vines bound together and carried as a small whip by the tallest of our three captors. The pain was intense. Blood ran from my forehead where thorns had ripped away skin. I shouted a curse and was immediately struck again. Now I held my tongue. This tall severe man bent from the waist and put his face very close to mine. Staring at me, he made it clear that no one was to speak. His language was different from ours but close enough to be understood. I heard his two companions call him Oland. Oland now held my life in his hands. Five of us were bound, chained together at the neck and a man named Oland would tell us if we were permitted to speak.

The three men moved about quickly preparing to travel. Six strong poles were cut and pigs were gutted. The sows and smaller pigs were lashed to the poles. The boar remained on the trail where he had died and was never touched. Oland and his men were following a familiar routine with hardly a word shared between them. They brought the five of us to our feet. In order for two of us to carry two poles loaded with meat, Mamout and I were now only bound together by our wrists with more chain between us allowing us to move the poles as needed. Our collar and ankle chains had been removed for travel. Another two of our group were chained together in similar fashion. Batou carried one pole on his own while his ankle chains remained in place. The boar was more than the group could easily carry so his bulk was left on the trail.

We were up and moving within two hours of our capture. Excitement I had felt hunting wild pigs seemed to have filled me in a previous life and died when I was brutally captured. Numb to everything, even the pain of my injuries, I was in shock. My plans, my ideas, my humor, concerns, imagination, music, colors, sounds, my name, all of it burned away as easily and completely as the early fog under a climbing sun. Gone, all of it gone. *Vordun*, who are you? *Vordun*, where do you live?

Mamout and I were carrying two poles and keeping pace as Oland's men led us north, up the river, on a difficult three hour march. My head was beginning to clear and I was suddenly very tired. It seemed my legs were refusing to work properly and the poles loaded with meat were cutting into my shoulders. Abruptly, Oland led us all off the trail into heavy cover. After a quick word to his two men he disappeared up the trail. The two men quickly replaced the restraints to our necks and ankles. They also made efforts to be sure we had water and bread from their supply. As we rested, Mamout and I were able to talk quietly. Mamout explained that Malek had died from his wounds just like the boar. His thigh had been sliced wide open by the tusks and he bled out quickly. Oland and his men had barely noticed him as they sorted out all that had been gathered in their net. Their only focus had been on living captives and dead pigs. Malek was probably still breathing as he was thrown from the trail down the slope under some small bushes. The huge boar was not worth the effort. By now, the first predators to reach the site would have tried to carry off what they could as they filled their stomachs. Scavengers and birds would be trying to grab some pieces as blood was in the air. As large a prize as the boar and Malek were, the forest would quickly claim them and pick them clean in the blink of an eye. Their bones would be scattered as mothers dragged off body parts to carry to their young but, eventually, all bones would settle on the floor of the bush to bleach under the West African sun. Another meal taken in the wild and all of those who ate would be out hunting to eat again while taking care not to become the eaten. An old story perhaps, but I was now reading from a new book.

Mamout whispered and explained that as the smaller pigs were speared, our men had come quickly down the trail to join the rest of us just as the boar charged into Malek. As the net was dropped on us, two of our men had continued forward and tried to help. They were quickly caught up in the struggle before being forced to surrender at the point of spears. The last of our group, Ganja, had hesitated on the trail and came no further. Mamout said he had glanced up the trail and caught a glimpse of Ganja's back as he ran away. Ganja was our least talented hunter, the least aggressive when tracking game. Now Ganja remained free. Oland and his two men had made no effort to go after him. The three slave hunters had risked a great deal by attacking a group of seven men. To capture five of us relatively free from injury required great skill and the element of surprise working in their favor. They were in no position to get greedy and divide their group in order to chase one man. Oland was thrilled to have captured five of us and he knew exactly what to do next. My mind was beginning to think again. I dared to hope that Ganja might be able to get help from our village and track us as we moved further north toward the tribes ruled by Agaja. Now I looked more closely at our two guards and began to think about the possibility of escape.

Just the thought of my village hurrying to organize a rescue attempt gave me some energy. After resting for a few hours, I tried to calculate our location and the distance back to our village. Then I heard voices and movement coming toward us from the north. The two men guarding us were obviously pleased to see Oland who was now accompanied by six other men. Oland was smiling broadly as he spoke to his two men. The six new men who had just arrived with Oland were carefully looking us over before hoisting the poles to their shoulders as they began to carry our meat back the way they had just come. Our captors quickly made certain our hands and necks were chained and we were on the move again. The pace was much faster now as the six new men were carrying the meat. This allowed Oland and his men to drive the five of us faster and further north. The trail Oland followed took us away from the river and moved us in a northwest direction. We marched a full hour at this pace and I assumed we were being taken to Oland's village. Then we turned to the west into a region I had never seen before. It was late in the afternoon when we were led to a small village. The few men and women of the village stopped to stare at us as we were pushed into a small fenced area. About a dozen goats and pigs raised by the village were kept inside the fence. We remained in our chains and were tied to small trees. Oland had been talking intently to a few men when he quickly came to the fenced area. About eight goats and eight pigs were herded out of the enclosure. Men from the village began to tie the animals together and lead them up a trail out of the village. Oland's two companions helped lead the animals along the path. Oland then struck out on the run moving out of sight up the trail. This was the last I ever saw of our "African brothers". Oland had surprised us in the early morning and had ruined our lives before the sun had set. Late that night I watched as the men from the village who had helped move the goats and pigs returned home without the animals. I then realized that the five of us had been sold. Five strong young men had been traded, used as currency for a small herd of goats and pigs. And the trading had only just begun.

Now change came quickly for the five of us. Held captive in the small village, we slept hard that night, curled up on the ground lying against one another. The worst day of our lives had left us empty. Five villagers had us up early and, after a meal of goat meat, we were moving further west. After two miserable days and nights we entered a large village. Two of the men that had been leading us went and sat with a small group of men under a large tree in the middle of a cluster of huts. Soon they all rose and the five of us were closely examined by the villagers and some of their wives. We were hungry, tired and sore from constant marching over the past four days. The beatings from being captured had left us cut and bruised. But the greatest pain that that each of us had to endure was our humiliation at being captured and sold as slaves. Once again, men were trading for us like we were pigs. After more talk, a small bag of stones that must have been gold nuggets was handed to the men who had brought us to this place. Just as quickly, they were gone headed back east. First traded for goats, we now had been sold for some gold. The amount was unknown to me and I did not care to know. In my new world, I was held by others and traded in the village marketplace which was beyond anything I could ever have imagined. My place in my home seemed forever gone. I was without a place. None of us had any idea where we were. The language spoken around us was not familiar to our ears. The idea that my father and men from our village could possibly find us and steal us back was now no more than a crazy dream. We were completely crushed and without hope.

Ten more days passed. Twice we slept in the same village for two consecutive nights. This meant we had two full days to rest. Otherwise we were chained together and on the move every day, always being pushed west. Mamout and I had begun this nightmare as good friends. Now we barely spoke. When you must stop, bend over and carefully position yourself so that the person chained to your neck does not shit on your feet as he squats next to a tree, you begin to focus on the worst features in each other. Yes, we were still friends but the shock and strain of this tragedy was tearing all of us to pieces. We tried to remind each other that we must be ready at the slightest opportunity to break away and try to escape but, in reality, our hope was disappearing with each passing day. The men who moved us were clearly experienced in their work. Our bindings were strong and constantly checked to be certain we were not working our hands or ankles free. We were fed better than I expected and regularly given water as these slave traders needed us alive and strong. While some captors were brutal in handling us, most were almost kind as they watched us pass through their world on the way toward the great water. These African men and women had bought and sold many others like the five of us. We had been raked out of the bush and bundled toward the great water. Regularly now we heard pieces of conversation about this great water, a large lake that they said had no end. Batou shook his head and doubted what we heard. How could there be such a lake where no man could see across to another side? I was tired and confused. I did not know what to believe. Our other two men were now almost silent. The two were chained together and terribly upset. Quiet and sad, their eyes were blank. They seemed weaker every day. From time to time, these two had simply sat on the ground and refused to move. Such rebellion was always dealt with by violence delivered immediately and with meaning. Even a relatively kind captor had nothing but pain to share when openly challenged by a slave. The slave had no standing, no voice, no meaning other than to obey. Captivity was like hunger – it drove men to try stupid things.

Batou and I had often enjoyed long talks together as we both had been speaking French since we were young. Our fathers had learned the language from traders who regularly met with elders from our tribe at a village four days journey to the southwest of our home. Batou and I, along with a few others in the village, spoke this French with our fathers and with each other. At first we did not realize that we were being trained to help lead our village as we grew older. Lead our village? Would we ever even *see* our village again?

Over the previous two days the land had become flat, no more rolling hills to climb. The soil was sandy, the air thick and we were now sweating all the time, even at rest. No amount of water to drink seemed enough. Dense jungle had slowed our pace. It seemed to rain at least twice every day, the rain always followed by a scorching sun that beat us down. The rags we wore around our waists, the only clothing we had, were filthy and always damp. Our captors rarely spoke, even to each other, but on this day they were speaking more often. The great water, it seemed that we were only one day's march from the great water. Now I watched them more closely. Changes were taking place and maybe, just maybe, we would have a chance to break away. Late in the day we arrived in a camp where about ten other people were gathered. For the first time in two weeks I saw people who looked like the five of us. Four men and two women with hands bound and chained at the neck, six other slaves.

The men who brought us in to camp now spoke with the guards who ran the camp. The six slaves we saw were chained to small trees inside a crude fence. There was a small shelter inside the pen, four poles supporting a flimsy roof of large jungle leaves and branches providing some shade and a spot of cover from the rain. The five of us were led to another pen about twenty yards away from the first one. The other slaves watched us with blank stares as we were chained inside our pen. Before I could turn my head to watch them, the men who had guarded us and marched us out from the bush over the past five days were gone back up the trail. New guards came and closely examined each of us. Particular inspection was made of our feet, our hands and our teeth. We were brought bowls of pig meat with rice, bananas and jugs of water. It seemed important to them that we could eat and drink what was given.

The next day little happened as we lay under the leaves and tried to sleep. We saw that the other slaves were just like us – silent, naked and tired. We could only shit and piss as far from our shelter as our chains allowed. The smell was foul. We quickly ate whatever food was given and this helped us sleep. Late in the day two guards entered the pen with a large bucket. They dipped out a clear palm oil which they poured over our shoulders. We were instructed to rub the oil over our arms and chest and to rub it on each other's back. More oil was poured into our cupped hands to cover our legs. We slept that night with full stomachs but anxious over what was to come.

My mother's name was Sanja. To her, I was always Yamar and on this night she walked with me in my sleep.

"Yamar, why do you stay so long on your hunt when you know your father has told you to return to the village after one night out on the trail?"

I reply, "Mother, all I want is to return home but I have been taken from our trails and no longer allowed to hunt. Men who only want me alive force me toward the great water. Stay with me for I no longer have a home."

My mother, who cannot understand, answers, "Do not be so foolish as to say you have no home. Turn to me now and take my hand as when you were small. It is time and your father will be missing us."

I want to turn and look for her as she moves into the fog.

Calmly I explain, "Dear Sanja, I have been made to face toward the great water and cannot be turned. If an egg is taken from the nest of the hawk, it cannot be returned. Be kind to me in your thoughts when you speak of Yamar."

Always in my dream she holds out her hand to lead me home and always I am forced to look away toward the great water. Always, I am turned west toward the great water.

The last day of our march began like the others. After meat and water our restraints were secured and we were moving west. Now six more slaves were marching in our line as we were driven forward. It was around noon with the sun directly over us when gulls that live near the great water began to appear.

Batou asked, "What is 'great water' supposed to mean? Why do these assholes push us for weeks just to move their slaves to some 'great water' anyway? It makes no sense to move us so far just to get to 'great water'. What's the damn point?"

I again told Batou what I had been saying for days. I did not know why or what this great water was about but it made no sense that we would be fed and guarded for so long if they planned to kill us. We could easily be dead many times over by now without going to such trouble.

"I don't know. My guess is that there is a big job to be done. Perhaps land by this great water needs to be cleared for a large village where huts and lodges are to be built. Maybe we will be put to work here in this area and can make a plan to escape." I tried to sound hopeful as we all grew more anxious.

By midafternoon the cries of the gulls were constant and our guards seemed to be in a hurry. Suddenly we were stopped and told to stand in line. Two guards hurried up the trail. Quickly the process from the day before was repeated as oil was poured on each of us. We were given water and soon the two who had gone forward returned with a man dressed in a fine blue robe. The garment went around his waist and was draped over his right shoulder. He looked at each of us closely as he slowly walked down the line. One of us he held by the chin as he tilted the head back and moved it from side to side. He squeezed some of us by the shoulder and opened mouths to study our teeth. This man placed his hand beneath the breasts of one of the women and moved them up and down.

The slave trader went about his inspection slowly and deliberately. He nodded to the guards. And then he spoke in the French;

"These young men are strong and will trade well. The women also have a good number of years left for work. We will get a good price."

Hurriedly now we were marched up the trail. I heard the great water long before I saw it. The roll of the surf on a calm day is rhythmic and pleasant. As we crested a series of large sand dunes my breath left me. I was awed by the beauty of it all. The blue-green sea, white foam on the waves, the white beaches stretching to both the north and the south were overwhelming. The water sparkled under a hot afternoon sun and I shaded my eyes. There would be no more marching to the west. Before us, to the west, the sea stretched forever. The sheer size of it was beautiful and frightening.

My mind seemed locked on one thought.

"I am Prince, a man forced out from Yoruba by his brothers, and I feel small like a single grain of sand on this beach."

We had no idea where we were going. We had no idea where we had been.

PRINCE of SAND - Chapter Two ... Les Hommes de la Mer / Men of the Sea

The boy had never known a parent and never had a friend. His memories of Newsham Orphanage in Liverpool were few. Coarse grey clothes, tight shoes and stern women working to keep too many little boys in line to eat, in line to go outside, in line to piss and shit, in line to come back inside, in line to get in bed. From a third floor dormitory window he could see the masts of the ships. This was his place. This was where he stood whenever he could escape the lines. Birds circled the docks. Sailors climbed the rigging of ships to work with the white sails. Men crawled around like ants moving cargo on and off the ships. But it was the ships themselves that gripped him and never let him go.

Billy Simms loved the sea. Indeed, he wanted to know all that he could about life at sea and everything he learned made him love it all the more. Simple in many ways and never having seen the inside of a school, the lad knew of nothing else and, although he would travel to many ports, he was never curious about anything else.

The first time Billy tried to run away he was quickly found at the docks. He was probably six or seven years old. Exact age is uncertain when everything related to your birth is unknown. Back in the orphanage, they pulled down his britches and whipped him. He was unfazed. His mind was on what he had learned, on a mistake he would not repeat, on how he could move three blocks from this place and make the docks his home.

"James Pinney … Robert Sterling … Billy Simms - off with your clothes and into the washtub."

Always the same order, always the same group - James Pinney … Robert Sterling … Billy Simms – it was as if the three boys shared the same long name. James Pinney … Robert Sterling … Billy Simms – every meal sitting on the same bench, every morning standing barefoot in night shirts at the foot of the bed they shared, every Saturday morning sharing the washtub, every evening kneeling together in front of their pew during devotions. Pinney and Sterling were inseparable. Billy Simms stood alone at the dormitory window.

Only a few more weeks passed and Billy was gone. The grey clothes of the orphanage had previously made it easy for others to spot him on the docks. He did not make the same mistake again. In a pile of cast-offs, he had seen a loose blue pullover and a blue pair of pants that someone from a church had left for the children. He hid them in a closet. Once away in his different clothes, he did not stop when he reached the docks. The Liverpool waterfront is enormous and seems to stretch forever. Billy did not know exactly where to go but he knew he needed to go far. This was an easy task for a boy who dreamed of exploring what he saw before him. He walked for hours along the waterfront, never stopping in one place for too long but never racing about as if on the run.

Long after he was a safe distance away, Billy rested on some crates near one of the ships. Three from her crew had stopped unloading for a few minutes to smoke their pipes. One older mate explained to the others,

"We was adrift in the doldrums, we was. Our coxswain had sailed before the mast. Already cranky when he had come on the boards, now, without even a fluky to stir the sails, the cut of his jib told you to leave him a wide berth."

Billy hardly understood a word, yet he could have sat listening to their banter all day. He knew enough to know they spoke of the sea and he knew he wanted more. Alone on the docks, Billy was not scared. Having been alone from birth, finding a place to sleep was challenging, not frightening. Looking intently at the buildings around him, Billy stared at the brick warehouse directly across the cobblestones from one of the ships. Two large sliding doors hanging on their track had been pushed shut secured with a large chain. He watched a rat scurry through the crack between the doors. Following close behind, Billy pried the doors apart enough for a skinny kid to squeeze through. Now inside, his eyes adjusting to dim light, he saw large sacks and crates stacked on the plank flooring. Rough timbers supported the roof above. He was hungry. Billy pulled on some crate lids but all were nailed shut. Large amounts of sugar and rice were stacked in heavy burlap sacks so there was no supper to be had there. Disappointed, but by no means beaten, Billy pissed in a corner before climbing up onto five sacks of sugar. He dropped his head on his arm and closed his eyes. The damp building was filled with a musty odor. Trying to rest, he was cold and getting colder. Climbing down to explore further, he got lucky. Half a dozen empty sacks were in a pile near a wall. Billy grabbed them and crawled back up onto his makeshift bed. One sack for a pillow, the others for cover and he was fast asleep.

Two men arrived at dawn. They unlocked the chain and the doors were pushed wide apart.

"Toby, listen to me, the King and Queen together would swim to China and back to taste me mum's pigeon pie! Have you not heard the song they're all singin'?

Sing, lads, sing for your supper.

No kissin' of the lass to make her cry.

Better to the table early with spoons at the ready

And one lucky lad will taste the pigeon pie!"

"Russell, Russell, stop squawkin' about pigeons in a pie. My missus sets me table with a royal mutton stew. Christ, the maharaja of bloody India once crawled on broken glass from Buckingham Palace to Dog and Duck Lane just to dig his spoon into Mrs. Williams mutton stew!"

They laughed easily as they began to sort crates and sacks into different piles. Wagons would soon be rolling up to the warehouses to start moving goods to different traders in Liverpool. Some freight stayed in the city. Most of it went to points north and east. Towns and coaching inns to the south were primarily supplied from London.

Toby Williams turned to his left, facing the rear of the warehouse, and stopped talking. He walked quickly to the timber support next to a five-sack pile of sugar. The stack came up to Toby's chest. There before him lay a sleeping child snuggled beneath a handful of burlap sacks.

"Russell, stop and come look. Blimey, we have a small visitor and damned if he isn't asleep on the sugar bound for Yorkshire!"

Billy would never understand just how his luck had changed that day. You could search Liverpool high and low and fail to find a kinder soul than ol' Toby Williams. Toby and his wife, Biddy, had lived in Liverpool for all of their fifty odd years. Toby found regular work on the docks, never going to sea except on the occasional short voyage to Ireland or France. His wife was a cook for the Tilson family, a family that had amassed their wealth by owning merchant ships and warehouses. Biddy and Toby had one child early in their marriage. The baby was stillborn, the delivery difficult for Biddy. There would be no more pregnancies for the good Mrs. Williams.

Toby gathered Billy in his arms before Russell could even ask him what he thought they should do with the boy. Billy was startled and began to try and wiggle free but Toby smiled, held him firm and said,

"No one is going to hurt you, lad. I am here to help."

After lowering him to his feet, Toby held Billy with a strong grip and smiled as he looked him over. Billy was on guard but this man was smiling when he could be cuffing him on the ear. Toby asked him if he was lost. How did he get into the warehouse? Was he trying to find his parents? Billy kept his mouth shut and stared at this old man holding his hand. Again, Toby smiled and then shrugged,

"I am a hungry man and I would wager the crown jewels that you are a hungry boy. Come now and we will find you a warm bowl of porridge."

If Billy was going to run, he quickly made up his mind to at least wait until he filled his growling belly. And then Billy Simms did something he could barely ever remember doing before. He smiled at another human being.

It made no difference to Toby that the boy refused to speak. After Billy ate a grown man's portion in the nearby tavern, Toby told Russell that he would be back soon. It was not far to the Tilson household where he took Billy around to the servants' entrance in the back. The cook, Mrs. Williams, was called to the door where she first laid eyes on Billy Simms. Husband quickly told wife what had taken place that morning. It made Toby feel good to watch Biddy melt before the lad as he knew she would. Quickly, she shooed Toby back to the docks as she gathered Billy up into the house and sat him in the corner of the kitchen. It was like Christmas, Easter and the king's birthday all coming at once, the thought of taking Billy home after work to share supper with her husband.

If asked, Billy would admit that Toby and Biddy Williams were always kind to him. Just the same, he chafed at their idea of home and their idea of his place in it. Mrs. Williams went through the motions and acted as if she was sincerely searching for the place that Billy had come from, the place that Billy refused to mention. But she was more than satisfied with his story that he was alone in this world. For Biddy, that implied that he wanted *someone* and *some* place in his life. Naturally, that place would be their tiny home and she would be the mother that Billy must yearn for. Soon enough, Toby realized that Biddy's heart, starving for a child, would be coldly denied once again.

Billy's new situation was acceptable to him for two reasons. He was constantly around his ships and he had a comfortable place to stay. Mrs. Williams cleaned him up and provided proper clothes. Food and a warm bed were offered and taken. Beyond that, Billy Simms made his regular rounds about the docks and nothing else mattered. The couple tried to discipline him into their dream of having a loving son being raised by loving parents. Biddy then tried to spoil him into her affections. Billy did not so much reject them as suffer them. The calico cat on the windowsill, he would be around and then he was gone.

Within months the boy was familiar with the basic language of men at sea. Ports of call, Liverpool schedules for in-bound and out-bound vessels, the rhythm of the tide, the hierarchy of a crew at sea, names and rigging for the different sails – Billy was born to go to sea. Why was this so? It would never occur to Billy to even ask such a question. Why do men breathe? Merchant ships and their crews became familiar to Billy and he to them. Soon he was regularly running errands for officers and crew, delivering an envelope to shipping offices or picking up something needed by a captain and carrying it back to the ship. Anything he could do to be a part of their world, this was Billy's mission. The halfpence he might earn meant nothing compared to the rare chance to come aboard and scamper about the ship itself.

In the spring of 1753 Captain Andrew Spencer Christopher brought his 150 ton schooner, the *Abundance*, up the mouth of the River Mersey and docked her neatly before striding down the gangway and onto the Liverpool docks. Billy Simms was at his elbow in a moment.

"Top of the mornin', Cap'n, sir. Cabin boy William Billy Simms at your service! The turn of the tide is due at twelve and ten. This south easterly should hold steady at one to two knots all day, Cap'n. Anything you need done on these docks today, anything at all, I am here to serve the best that I can, thank you kindly, sir."

Captain Christopher would, in fact, be quite busy this day. He needed to locate the offices of Hardy & Tilson, obtain the necessary signatures on his bill of lading, confirm that the cargo of sugar, rice and tobacco bound for Le Havre would be brought aboard tomorrow beginning at dawn and, if he was lucky, find one more crew needed for this Channel crossing. Le Havre, the closest port to Paris, was home to important clients of the owners of the *Abundance*. Before brushing away this rather amusing snot nosed wharf rat, he glanced down at Billy and asked,

"Boy, might you be able to tell me where to find the offices of Hardy & Tilson?"

Billy damn near jumped out of his shoes and quickly said,

"Cap'n sir, indeed I could tell you, yes sir, but it should be my pleasure to lead you there to Hardy & Tilson me-self. So, if you please and with your permission, Cap'n, please follow me."

And with that the boy was off. Head down, shoulders square, Billy marched Captain Christopher up three blocks and over two leading him with focused determination.

"Move aside, sir, if you please, the Captain is passing through." ... "Step lively there mate, the Captain is out on business this morning."

Billy barked orders at grown men and women alike in his efforts to clear the way for the good Captain C who had to hurry just to keep pace with this salty lad. As the years unfolded, Billy would often think to himself,

'I do believe I get more out of Captain C than Captain C gets out of me.'

If true, he must have taken quite a lot from the relationship for Billy would always give the Captain his all, his very best. Before the day was out Billy had managed to move even the thoughtful and deliberate Captain Christopher.

"Cap'n, if I was to be cabin boy on your run to Le Havre you could see just how handy I can be aboard ship, sir. Please, your honor, one chance for Billy Simms and you will never regret it. I can promise you that, sir."

Captain C had to admit it. This determined youngster had helped make this day in

Liverpool a particularly productive one given his astonishing knowledge of the docks and the locals working there. Still, he was young for a cabin boy. He turned to face Billy,

"Master Simms, as the position for cabin boy aboard the *Abundance* is currently open and in recognition of your generosity extended to both Captain and crew this day, you will be offered a berth for the Le Havre voyage upon satisfaction of a single condition."

Billy was light headed as he responded, "Oh Captain Christopher, please tell me what it is that needs to be done! You are the best of men, sir! Please Captain, what must I do?"

"Simms, this is 1754 and we operate our ship in modern times. The *Abundance* is no kidnapper of youth and you are but ten years old. Have your guardian present to discuss permission for you to come aboard for this trip to France. If granted, you are to report for duty at dawn. You are dismissed, Master Simms."

Billy stood as tall as he could in front of the Captain. Without speaking, he looked directly into his face for what seemed a long time. Then, in his clearest and strongest voice, he answered,

"Aye-aye, Captain."

When he found Toby at the warehouse the discussion was brief,

"There is really nothing for talk, sir. I be needin' your permission for Cap'n Christopher. I am cabin boy of the *Abundance,* ordered to board her at dawn. Without permission, I'll be up with the dawn to find another ship, another cap'n. The *Abundance*, she is a fine ship, Mr. Williams. I will be takin' me orders from the good Captain C. Please sir, will you be followin' me back to the *Abundance*?"

Actually, Toby agreed with Billy Simms. Billy and his call to the sea would not be denied. There was nothing to be gained by delay. Toby joined Billy in the Captain's stateroom within the hour. Toby made a point of asking where Billy would bunk and asked to see that area of the crew's quarters. He was pleased that Captain Christopher handled himself as a gentleman.

Little was said between the two as Toby and Billy walked home for the meal that Biddy was preparing. Toby was forming the explanation he would share with his wife. The new cabin boy of the *Abundance* was living his dream with his mind halfway across the Channel. Permission had been granted. Billy would sail to Le Havre and return to Liverpool. But Billy and Toby both knew that, as Billy went to sea, his returns to port would be few and far between. It was 1753 and Billy, now nine or ten years old, was taking his place among men of the sea.

For two days Billy helped prepare the *Abundance* for her Le Havre journey, his maiden voyage. Hard chores such as stacking freight and scrubbing decks were on the list of thankless tasks he was ordered to perform. The boy had never known such joy. Exploring every nook of the ship, from the hold up into the yards, he worked from dawn until the grown men of the crew stopped to sleep. After crawling onto his hammock, he was up again with the dawn ready to scrub any surface as ordered. Billy loved the *Abundance*. She would be the mother he never knew and cabin boy Simms would do anything, absolutely anything, Captain Christopher ordered to be done. Furthermore, in his mind, he would be the best cabin boy on the high seas or kill himself trying.

The weather was fair with a favorable breeze blowing that afternoon. Captain C gave orders on the rising tide that took the *Abundance* out into and down the channel of the Mersey. Heading west toward Dublin, they would turn south sailing through St. George's Channel before rounding Penzance and Plymouth on the southwest point of their island nation. Through the night they planned to stay on an east by southeasterly course, scheduled to make Le Havre on the coast of France the next evening.

Billy was busy with the errands for a ship under sail. The cook in the galley barked orders cluttered with curses that Billy did not even pretend to understand. All of the many references to his mother caused him to giggle to himself. Of course, he had never known a mother yet this cook went out of his way to describe her in the most amusing ways! At least two of the crew always remained on duty. Billy carried food in a bucket from the galley to the forecastle where a seaman would eat. Running messages from Captain C to first mate and crew took him back and forth across the ship. And the decks, Captain C had an odd passion for keeping every deck surface scrubbed. It seemed as if emeralds and diamonds must have been scattered just beneath the surface and the good captain was determined to scrub away the top of the deck to uncover this hidden fortune. And as Billy tried to take it all in, the cook bellowed from below,

"Cabin boy to the galley ... NOW! And move your miserable arse quicker than shit through a goose or your whore of a mother will be sweepin' ya off the rocks below Dover!"

As Billy happily raced to the galley, he tasted blood as he bit his lip hard to keep from laughing out loud.

It was around four in the morning as the first watch ended when a gale unexpectedly began to blow out of the northeast. Gusts reached fifty knots and seas of ten feet and more were rolling. The Captain had been alerted and was topside. The squall that came on the gale dumped a cold rain now lashing the crew sideways as Captain Christopher ordered the *Abundance* into the wind,

"North by northeast .... head her into the wind, Mr. Olson."

Helmsman Olson's practiced response came in cadence, "Aye-aye, Captain, ... north by northeast."

The crew of the *Abundance* was on full alert as they took to their stations, yet they went about their tasks with practiced ease. Billy watched intently as this bizarre jig was danced to the trumpet of the sea. Fear was the last thought to cross his mind. Respect for the sea? Certainly. But no fear was present as the crew made the ship as safe as she could be in these conditions. Sail was being reduced as the Captain put the men through their paces. Billy recognized the cook's voice, heard above the others, as he cursed the storm most roundly. One of the crew, Mr. Jones, was on deck as ordered with a replacement line needed to secure the mainsail where one shroud was blowing free in the wind. At that moment, a plunging breaker hit her midship from the port side. The *Abundance* rolled violently to starboard sending Billy tumbling across the deck and slamming into the bulkhead.

Captain C called out, "Down the Mainsail! Up the Trysail! Jones, hitch that line to the cabin boy and secure him with the closest belaying pin to starboard!"

"Aye-aye, Captain.

Jones went straight to Billy who had regained his feet by clutching one of the grab rails. Jones' strong hands hitched the line securely under Billy's arms allowing him free movement without being wrenched about the waist. Billy thought he felt a rough hand tousle his hair as Jones moved to secure the other end of the line with a belaying pin as ordered. A rogue wave slammed the *Abundance*, again from port. She lay hard over to starboard. Billy could reach out and touch the sea. In that moment

Billy and two others saw seaman Tom Jackson as he was swept from the rigging and

into the sea. No thought crossed Billy's mind.

He simply jumped into the ocean.
Head up, paddling furiously, Billy
tried to look straight ahead in the
direction that Jackson had been
taken. He managed to crest the swell
in front of him. As he rose well above
the ship, he peered into the trough
and spotted Jackson dead ahead. He
sped down the backside of this wave
as another crested and he was
forced under the foam. Still paddling,

he came up spitting salt water as he tried to find Jackson through blurry eyes. He was
aware of the line secured under his arms and this helped calm him. Seaman Jones,
having thrown the overboard pole toward Jackson, was calling out in a loud and
steady voice. Jackson, a strong swimmer, managed to keep his head above the
surface, waiving his arms when he could. Billy bobbed around like a cork.
He was not yet more than seventy pounds and the storm tossed him about across the

waves. Coming off the back of the next wave, he was within Jackson's reach. Jackson held the boy by his shoulders and immediately realized that Billy was tied to a line. Grabbing the line with his right hand, Jackson swung Billy over his shoulder and screamed over the wind as he ordered him to grab him by the neck with both of his hands,

"Dig your hands into me and hold for all you are worth! Do you hear me, boy? Don't let me neck loose for nothin'!"

Jackson pulled in some line and looped the slack under his own arms. He felt the line pulled taut as Jones began to take in line from the ship's end. Just that quickly, the emergency passed. Tom Jackson was brought safely back onto the *Abundance* with Cabin Boy Simms hanging on his neck tight as a leach. All continued their work as the *Abundance* weathered the storm. Captain Christopher returned to his stateroom as he ordered Billy to join him there.

The Captain, looking over the soaked cabin boy who carried a wide-eyed gaze of adventure on his young face, spoke softly,

"Master Simms, before retiring to quarters for dry clothes and this watch to your bunk, let me make clear one of my laws at sea. You are ordered to remain on ship at all times, unless under my direct order to do otherwise. Do you understand, Master Simms?"

As was his practice, Billy looked him square in the eye and answered clearly,

"Aye-aye, Captain."

"Be off with you then. Report back to me one hour into third watch after pulling a mug of warm tea from the galley."

Billy was turned and headed for the door when he heard Captain Christopher finish,

"And Master Simms, you have brought honor upon yourself and upon the *Abundance* this night. On behalf of Mr. Jackson, this crew and all men of the sea, welcome aboard."

PRINCE of SAND - Chapter Three ... Trahison d'un Village / Betrayal of a Village

Imprisoned with a growing number of victims, men and a few women who, like me, had been captured and kidnapped from villages further inland, I was still confused and fearful as to why we were being held in this filthy camp by the big water. It was now September in this year of 1760. We had been eight weeks as prisoners. Waves reaching the shore were relentless. I could hardly remember what it had been like to wake up without waves breaking on the shore. Sixteen years I had lived on the high plain in Dahomey. Now these surroundings by the sea had become my normal. Batou and the others still called me Prince. It had become my name and would follow me the rest of my life, but I did not feel like a prince.

Miserable days had stretched into weeks. The five of us had waited to learn our fate. We were put to work daily building huts in the slave village where we were held captive. The men who had hurried us out of the bush and through the jungle to the coast were gone and returned to the bush. The slave trader, Diallo, always in his fine blue robes and sandals, gave orders to his men who guarded us with their spears and whips.

Diallo ran his camp of prisoners for one purpose – to sell and trade Africans as slaves to captains of ships and other African slavers for the best deal that he could get. This camp was one of a number that were strung along an area between the town of Annamaboe and the beach. Each cluster of huts had a slaver, someone like Diallo, who bought the men, women and children that were brought out of the bush by different suppliers. These slavers worked to keep their captives alive until they could be sold onto the ships. Their system worked well enough as long as slavers and prisoners alike could be protected from area tribes that might send raiding parties to capture or steal from weak slavers.

Along this stretch of West African slaving coast, the most powerful slaver who provided protection was called Jaja. Lord Jaja was a large man of large appetites. Over three hundred pounds, this dealmaker wore silk purple robes trimmed in gold. He was carried about in a large chair secured to strong poles that his four handlers carried on their shoulders. Jaja had once been a trader like Diallo but Jaja was not satisfied being one of many. Jaja planned to control this trading of slaves over as large an area of the shore as possible. So, in a cutthroat world controlled by cheaters and thieves, Jaja became the biggest cheater and most dangerous thief of all.

Early one morning we were awakened as a new cluster of prisoners were herded into our enclosure. Particular attention was drawn to an enormous warrior from the Mandinka tribe. Without a doubt, he was the strongest man I had ever seen. He was joined with a woman and their two children. In small groups, we were taken out of our chains and separated from one another. Batou and I exchanged a nervous glance as we were separated for the first time since our capture. Just as quickly, I was fastened at the neck and the ankle to a man who would quickly teach me the truth – the truth of my wretched enslavement. This man, a Muslim, was called Abdul-Barry.

Abdul-Barry was the son of an important man from a village not far from the big water. Educated in Arabic, he also spoke some of the French. We were always guarded in conversation, but Abdul-Barry had very little to say to me anyway. He was disgusted to be chained to a tribe member like me and he was shocked to learn that I also spoke some of the French. In brief conversations, my eyes were opened to horrors of a slave trade that I never could have imagined. Abdul-Barry's father owned many slaves himself and, from time to time, he sold slaves to Jaja. Ten days earlier, Abdul-Barry had been sent to Annamaboe by his father with specific instructions to sell eight slaves and return home with the gold coins earned from the sale. He was to initially contact a trader friendly to his father. But as many other eighteen year old young men, Abdul-Barry was excited to be in town, to be on his own and he had his own ideas about selling his slaves. On the verge of tears, he explained, "My father sent two of his guards with me to handle the slaves. I was certain I could bargain for a better price and impress my family as a skillful trader. We arrived in town. I sent one of the guards to a tavern where many hard men gathered to drink and discuss the slave trade. I was stupid to trust him with such an important job."

Quickly, Abdul-Barry's guard was noticed by some of Diallo's men as he bragged of having eight slaves for sale that he and his boss would be selling to the right buyer. Diallo's men were trained to find and prey on the weak. Abdul-Barry looked sadly at Prince, "My guard was fed meat and rum. He was taken to a room where a woman was given to him. Two of Diallo's men returned with him and all three of them begged me to quickly bring the slaves to their location. It was promised that a handsome price would be paid. It seemed to be a perfect arrangement. We followed these men into a hut on the beach with my father's slaves in their chains. As we entered the dark hut, my first guard was cut down before my eyes. Two men stepped out of the dark and plunged a spear into his throat. I was quickly grabbed and chained to the other guard. In that moment, we were now a group of ten slaves and hardly a word had been spoken."

Jaja, Diallo and other traders gathered slaves as opportunities came along. They tried to attract and win favor with the most reliable suppliers of prisoners from the inland regions. If you could get first look, arrange the opportunity to screen those recently captured and purchase the best of them, you would first build a supply of strong young men with many years of labor remaining in their limbs. Next, you would mix in young women and children old enough to work. Now you could trade with the European ship captains who anchored their foul smelling slave ships out in the harbor. Jaja was an aggressive trader who favored one supplier over all others, a brutal warlord called Nimba. More than once, Jaja and Nimba had targeted entire inland tribes to be attacked and kidnapped to this coastal prison. Together they planned and executed the crimes of murder and larceny on such a scale that the entire west coast of Africa took notice.

As so often the case in achieving great success, the timing of their best plan was perfect. Within one day's march from the sea was a small tribe led by a young tyrant named Char. Jaja had known Char's father, Dambi. He had bought prisoners from Dambi in earlier years. So it had come as a surprise to Jaja when he learned of Dambi's death and that his son, Char, now led the warriors of their tribe. Nimba led some of his men into the region and brought back his report to Jaja,

"This Char is blind with power and murdered his own father. Two of his men walked with Char into Dambi's hut in the middle of the night. Char ordered the men to cut his father's throat. His blood was collected in bowls and mixed with the blood of pigs. Dambi's hands and feet were cut away and laid out next to parts cut from animals and serpents. His people fear Char greatly."

Jaja stared at Nimba and asked, "How many are in his tribe?" "About two hundred fifty live with Char", answered Nimba. Jaja replied,

"What do we know about this Char? He is new at leading this tribe and his people fear a man who cut his own father's throat. I believe Dambi was a decent leader. No worse than these others who bring their captives out to this shore to trade for cloth, beads and the iron bars that they take back to their villages. I wonder if this Char can so easily cut his father to pieces and then wear his robes?"

The two men decided that Jaja was someone Char needed to meet. Nimba would be the messenger to invite Char to come and learn of their growing slave trade. Messengers were sent to advise Char that Nimba and a small group of his men would be coming to his village for the purpose of extending an invitation. Efforts were made to flatter the new leader. The message was one of praise for his new position and of Jaja's desire to develop friendly trade with Char, the leader of his tribe. The plan by Jaja and Nimba to double-cross this rogue murderer, Char, was underway.

As Nimba made arrangements to bring Char to Jaja's huts, Jaja was meeting with Captain Roux who had brought his French slave ship, the *Cramoise*, into the harbor two weeks earlier. Sailing out of Marseilles, Captain Pierre Roux and the *Cramoise* had run afoul of Barbary pirates passing through the Straits of Gibraltar. Moroccan pirates had demanded a toll for the ship's safe passage. Roux had refused and made a run for the freedom of the open seas. Unsuccessful, he and his crew were forced to dock the ship in Casablanca as negotiations for a ransom ensued. In addition to the gold coins eventually paid, Roux lost just over a month bottled up in Casablanca. Arrogant and impatient on his best day, Captain Roux was rude in his manner with Jaja,

"Critical, it is critical that the *Cramoise* be given every priority in obtaining a full load of your slaves! We *must* be in Trinidad before the end of November. Those fools in Casablanca cost me weeks of delay! I will see those bastards hang from the yardarm of a French battleship of the line, but that must come later. Monsieur Jaja, when will we be full? I must have a minimum of three hundred slaves in the hold. When, Jaja, when can we sail?"

Jaja, raising his hands to Roux and moving back in his chair, smiled slightly as he shrugged his shoulders, "Please, please, Captain. You know that I am always at your service, but three hundred slaves? Your ship will be full, Captain Roux, but such a large cargo does not just walk up onto the beach ready to load. But do not be so upset, Captain. You are at the right place. I can tell you that Nimba and I know of your schedule and we have a plan that can help all of us if we work together. Soon, Captain, soon we will be ready to share details. But first, prepare the *Cramoise* to be unloaded beginning tomorrow. Clear your decks, Pierre, and empty the hold. Nimba and his warriors may have a large group of slaves assembled sooner than you can imagine."

What could he say? Captain Roux looked at Jaja and shook his head. The fact that he and his crew were so dependent on these traders of slaves was almost more than he could stomach. No captain trusted the traders and the slavers knew that these captains were liars and cheats competing among themselves to see who could steal the most from the traders. This distrust made for unpleasant negotiations but true discomfort, the friction that drove all players in this evil business to always be on their guard, evolved from the reality of a human cargo. Sacks of sugar do not rise up in the night to rip a sailor limb from limb. The stack of iron bars and rods to be unloaded from the hold do not contaminate others on board with yellow fever or dysentery. Humans were traded for the single reason that the profits to be made were huge. In an open market, the profits are large when the risks are great. Jaja, Pierre, Nimba and the others, they danced a dangerous dance and they learned to watch their partners closely. Men who survived many years trading slaves were few.

Nimba and Jaja remained after Roux had returned to the *Cramoise*. They spoke at length,

"Nimba, this French ass almost went too far tonight. I look forward to cutting out his tongue as he watches the knife pass before his eyes. But tell me, how is our plan for Char coming together?"

Nimba nodded slowly as he prepared to answer, "You are right. This Char is going crazy to be treated as someone important. We need only to continue to rub this prick with a big promise and he will come to the trap panting like a dog. Char is so anxious to become our partner that I fear he will make his moves too obvious."

Jaja listened and stared out of the doorway that faced the ocean. Soft yellow light spilled out onto the beach. The full moon brought the high tides and the waves were washing up close to the hut. September brought a slightly cooler breeze in the evening and Jaja often stayed up late enjoying some relief from the constant heat. "Yes, try to keep the fool calm. He will agree to anything that makes him look like a king but he must be controlled. Once he has played his role, our work will be easier. Let me know how I can help keep him in place. When will you next bring him to me?"

Nimba rose to his feet, tired and ready to go to his own hut, "Tomorrow night. Char is in love with the plan and is anxious to hear you confirm the timing. Unless you want to delay, I will bring him tomorrow night."

Jaja nodded in agreement, "No reason for delay. The plan is sound. Bring the lamb to the altar. Have your men ready and we will move soon."

Four days passed and Captain Roux was beside himself. The *Cramoise* cargo of cloth, iron bars, tools and beads was unloaded with help from Jaja's men. This morning Captain Roux was searching for Jaja to demand his commitment for delivering hundreds of slaves. Without asking permission, he barged into Jaja's meeting place completely ignoring all others present,

"Monsieur Jaja, my ship floats empty in the harbor. Empty! Today, Jaja, loading slaves must begin today or I am forced to find other slavers to fill the hold!"

Jaja, who was meeting with the trader Diallo, was incensed by such blatant rudeness but hid it well. Nodding slightly in apology to Diallo as he departed, Jaja turned his attention to the Frenchman,

"Captain, I was just sending my man to fetch you. As promised, Nimba and I have excellent news for you. In fact, today we will begin loading the *Cramoise*. Tell your crew to be ready to receive fifty, mostly men, and .."

"*Fifty*?" Roux screamed, "Fifty is a pitiful number and not nearly enough! Good god, you ignorant ape, have you not understood what I have been telling you?"

Roux was terribly wrong to show such disrespect for Jaja. He would pay for his arrogance in ways he could not imagine. In one glance the Captain saw the dark side of this ruthless trader of flesh and he physically recoiled. Narrowed eyes cut into him as Jaja snapped his head around with chin down and his jaw drawn tight as a vice. It seemed as though the words were being spat from Jaja's mouth as he hissed,

"Roux, shut your damn mouth long enough to hear what is happening and listen well. Fifty is the number you will receive *today*. Tomorrow, Captain, within the next twenty-four hours, your crew must manage another two hundred fifty slaves in a single loading. The first group of fifty has been collected in our huts over many weeks and they will be loaded this afternoon. For tomorrow, one entire village has been targeted and is being surrounded by Nimba's warriors as we speak. Roux, we will roll these people up like stacks of wood and deliver them in our longboats. Just be damned sure you and your crew can hold up your end. Do not, I repeat, do not fuck this up. Such a large group must be handled with brute strength and great skill."

Captain Roux actually shivered when he met Jaja's stare. He was not intimidated by many men but the sudden reversal in Jaja's manner, brought on by Roux's own asinine behavior, left the captain on the defensive. Clearly, the Jaja now before him was not a man to cross. Finally, Roux managed a few words,

"Beg your pardon, sir. That is wonderful news, wonderful. My nerves have been on edge and I apologize for my shortcomings. The *Cramoise* will look forward to the arrival of fifty prisoners this afternoon. Now I must hurry to gather my crew to begin preparations for a total of three hundred slaves on board by tomorrow night. Jaja, I am in your debt. Good day, sir."

Captain Roux was physically relieved to be out of Jaja's sight. He told himself he would need to find another trader further down the coast for his next slaving voyage. There was no mistaking the look of pure hatred that had flashed in Jaja's eyes and the captain knew that he had brought some of this on himself. It would be a blessing to soon be underway on the deck of the *Cramoise* as she set sail outward bound for Trinidad.

Jaja took a long pull from a jug of rum on a side table and calmed himself. Roux was a pain and he would be dealt with soon enough, but Jaja had allowed his emotions to spill forward. Perhaps women in the villages gathering their goats could practice such behavior but not men in Jaja's world. To lose control, even briefly in a conversation, was to allow a potential enemy to see inside your soul. Men who paid attention when such insight was offered were men to watch out for in the future. Control. Jaja was always working to gain and maintain control. You work so hard to be in control. Only fools then lose what was so hard earned. He was many things, but Jaja was no fool.

Now Jaja sat and reviewed the plan details with a senior lieutenant. Nimba was with his men and would be leading them into position after midnight tonight. The village would be under siege around four in the morning. They hoped to have the first thirty to forty prisoners brought out to the beach before noon. Using longboats that held about twenty-five captives, they would begin rowing these slaves out to the *Cramoise* and continue throughout the day. As they discussed the details, Diallo returned to finish his business with Jaja,

Diallo spoke, "Jaja, the fifty slaves in my huts can be delivered at anytime. The price that is set is agreeable to me. My men will pick up the iron bars and tools that we agreed to. When do you want the prisoners brought to your boats?"

"My men will be ready to take possession shortly after noon. I ask that we leave your restraints on these fifty and I will have replacement bindings delivered to your huts as soon as we can", responded Jaja.

"Certainly. There is no hurry on new bindings. Jaja, call on me for help if needed. The fifty will be on the beach at noon", answered Diallo.

By noon all fifty of us held by Diallo had been herded as one to the beach. Another few captives from Jaja's huts were marched to the same spot. The first longboat, manned by six oarsmen and the helmsman, was filled with twenty-five captives.

Abdul-Barry and I, locked together at both neck and ankle, were in the second load. Months had passed since our capture. My feet remained sore after forced marches over hundreds of miles. Now, after staring at the great water, after living at the foot of the waves, after trying to imagine what the ships in the harbor must be like, now the time had come. I was chained in a boat being moved over waves as men quickly rowed me toward one of these ships - the three masts of the *Cramoise*. My mind was racing. You think you are ready for what is coming next. Now it was time. And yet I had no idea what was coming next. *Vordun, where do you live?*

We were rowed to the side of the ship. It towered above us. How could anything so large stay up on top of water? Touching it was frightening. Men, black men and foul smelling white men, pushed us toward the middle of the enormous ship. At the back of the ship a section of the deck was pulled up to serve as a shield. Whenever male slaves were pushed from the lower level up onto the deck this shield, this barricado as the sailors called it, was always pulled up. Members of the crew and some of Jaja's men stood protected behind the barricado. Some were manning swivel guns that allowed a few to control many. The message was clear and reinforced at every turn. Attempting to attack the men that ruled the ship was a dangerous choice to make. The barricado had extensions preventing attackers from coming around the sides. Nets around the perimeter of the *Cramoise* told the desperate that jumping off the ship was no solution. Once on deck, we were just as quickly forced below decks into a space that prevented anyone taller than four feet to stand erect. This dark and damp hole slammed anyone climbing aboard with the foulest odors a body should have to endure. So revolting, only rotting flesh could compare. At least half of our group of fifty vomited, our stomachs turned in involuntary spasms. The human waste, the sweat and vomit, it all swirled together bringing tears to our eyes that made the mix complete. By design this space was cramped, but for fifty we could arrange ourselves to lie down together on the shelves we shared. Little did I know that three hundred of us would be claiming these very shelves within the next twenty-four hours.

Char believed that Jaja and Nimba were moving forward with their plan on land. Days earlier, Jaja and Nimba had seduced Char with visions of power and wealth. After we were loaded onto the *Cramoise*, night fell with Nimba's men surrounding Char's tribe. The dawn brought those people their total ruin. Char had led them through a long night of ritual celebration. All were shocked and totally unprepared to awaken to the spears held by Nimba's men. Char, dragged from his hut by warriors holding him by each arm, snatched himself free and rushed directly toward Nimba screaming with rage. Easily grabbed by others from the raiding party, they laughed as they rudely ran Char out of the village and into the surrounding jungle. Char's voice was no longer heard. And then terrible screams rose above the confusion. The cries of an animal under slaughter are both authentic and unmistakable. Char's handlers jogged back into the village, without Char, and dropped two severed hands and two feet in front of Nimba. Women and men of the tribe dropped to their knees. Greatly afraid, they began to wail and raise their cries to *Vordun*. Protection, holy wrath, revenge, mystical intervention and forgiveness – they called on their gods and their spirits from their knees. This tribe, crushed and confused, fell into line and marched toward the coast as ordered by Nimba and his men. It seemed that Char, their leader, had joined his father in a violent death.

My first night on a ship passed for me with no sense of night or day. Suffering, shared human suffering in a state of chaos, was all I remembered. Normal activities such as sleeping, waking, eating, drinking, standing and speaking were no longer normal. We were under strict orders not to speak but no member of any crew would patrol this slice of hell and voices murmured constantly. Moans of despair were mixed in with whispered questions and chants to *Vordun*. Later, as light filtered below the deck, I stared around and hung my head. People that yesterday appeared somewhat normal seemed to have aged many years. It occurred to me that I was no longer sixteen. In the middle of the day we were ordered up onto deck. Shielding our eyes from a full sun, white crew and Jaja's black warriors told us to jump about the deck as guards behind the barricado stood behind the swivel guns. Jump around? Why? What were they saying? Later we realized that slave captains had learned that some form of daily exercise helped bring better prices for their cargo. Jumping around the deck increased cargo value. Therefore we jumped.

Ordered to stop, we took cups of a thin gruel and were gulping down this only meal when I saw one of the longboats being rowed toward the *Cramoise*. Hurriedly we were shoved below. Soon the first group of twenty-five tribe members joined us in our hell. Within an hour, another twenty-five, and then another, and another. Fuck.

The hundreds of slaves being crammed with us below deck were from a tribe led by some man called Char. The frightened captives had only been captured earlier that day and they were totally confused. They said that their leader had been carried out of the village and murdered. Screams had been heard and their captors had laughed as a pair of hands and feet were thrown onto the ground. The last load of slaves was up on deck. No way. I thought there was no way another load could possibly be crammed into this space. Suddenly, the process was reversed. Hundreds of us collected below were now ordered above. Gulping fresh air, I looked around a crowded deck as the sun was getting low over the sea. Shots rang out. Some signal had been given and Jaja's warriors fell on the suddenly betrayed crew. The captain of the ship, called Captain Roux, was the first to fall as a spear was driven into his back. Within minutes crew members were either bleeding out on a slippery deck or begging for their lives as they lay in the bloody mess, face down with hands stretched out above their heads. Jaja's men had taken control of the *Cramoise* when the last man from the longboat, a man called Char, climbed aboard and stepped onto the deck. The collective gasp of over two hundred fifty frightened prisoners rolled over the ship like a wave. People closest to Char backed away as a crescent shaped space was cleared before him. Wherever he turned or walked, this space of fear and amazement radiated from him. Char was alive? His hands and feet that everyone thought had been chopped off in the village were there to be seen. *Vordun*, where do you live?

The warrior called Nimba moved to Char's side smiling and put an arm on his shoulder. Now some men of the tribe were on their feet and shouting with excitement. Freedom! Freedom? Others from Nimba's ranks called out in the French,

"Oui, liberte!" "Yes, you are free! Everyone gather yourselves and move to the sides of the ship. Climb into the longboats carefully when you are called. Your chains will be removed when we reach the shore where we have the necessary tools. Sit and try to relax now. We will work to clean this bloody deck."

FREE! *FREE?* I could not understand. We were slaves held for sale. Who is talking about being free? Why? Three longboats were now alongside the *Cramoise*. Quickly the bodies of Captain Roux and his murdered crew were lowered into one boat. Next, the group of us from Diallo's huts began to be loaded. The few surrendered members from Roux's crew were mopping the deck. Having been ordered to get to work, they were grateful to still be alive and jumped to the task with great energy. Nimba and his men stayed close to the exuberant Char who marched among his tribe relishing his role as lord and savior. To anyone that would listen, Char bragged as to how he and Jaja had directed Nimba and his men to destroy Captain Roux and his foreign crew. But first, it had been helpful to have Roux empty his valuable cargo that would now enrich their tribe. Only by deceiving the *Cramoise* could this attack be so successful. Char called out to his tribe,

"Your nightmare was brief but necessary! I order that it be removed from your minds! All is well. As your king, I command that no harm shall come to you!"

We were in the longboats and pulling for the shore. I looked up. Suddenly we had turned. After drawing near the beach we had angled toward another ship in the harbor. Soon we were brought alongside. I gazed around and saw the name of the ship. We were boarding a British slave ship, the *Nelly*. The well-armed men loyal to Nimba were no longer speaking about anyone being "free". These soldiers were not speaking at all. All of us in chains were now being hurried out of the longboats and loaded onto the *Nelly*. Nimba's men had one job to complete and one job only – move three hundred chained slaves out of the longboats and safely turn them over to the crew of the *Nelly*.

Jaja and Nimba had made their plan and with careful execution the scheme had worked perfectly. Char had been manipulated and led to believe that helping Nimba deliver his tribe of two hundred fifty villagers to the French ship *Cramoise* would result in his sharing in the spoils when Nimba and Jaja captured the *Cramoise* after killing her crew. Char participated in the charade as hands and feet were brutally hacked off of a slave whose screams convinced the villagers that Char had been murdered. The traumatized village had then followed Nimba's orders to proceed to the waiting *Cramoise*. Char loved being dramatically brought out onto the deck to lead his amazed and superstitious tribe back into the longboats. He was particularly pleased to be part of the deadly trick played upon the murdered French captain as the *Cramoise* was captured. Char continued to smile even as the longboats were diverted to the waiting *Nelly*. As Char was about to step onto the deck of the Nelly, he turned to his "partner", Nimba, to ask why the longboats had not rowed directly to the shore. It never occurred to Char that he had been so skillfully betrayed. At that moment, Nimba stepped aside as one of his strongest warriors held his battle-axe firmly in two hands. The axe was raised to shoulder height as the man stepped forward pivoting on his left foot and swung the axe in a wide level arc. Char's severed head bounced twice in the longboat as his twitching body slumped with blood spurting from the neck. Just as quickly, the body was slipped over the side providing a generous meal for a few well located sharks. For weeks, Char's head rested high on a pole after Jaja had secured the *Cramoise*. Jaja stripped the cannon from the ship and had them cemented into position to help protect the harbor. He kept the vessel in his 'protection' sending word to her owners in Marseilles that he would wait for them to make claim for their ship. Jaja released his 'official' version of what had taken place. All were advised that Char and members of his tribe had traveled to the shore and boarded longboats. These 'pirates' then proceeded to board the *Cramoise* under false pretenses murdering the captain and crew. This lawless behavior would not be tolerated by the European captains and slave brokers of the Gold Coast. Jaja had immediately sent Nimba and his men to subdue Char and his thieves. Char was killed in battle and his tribe was quickly sold into bondage to Captain Christopher of the *Nelly*. Char and Captain Roux, the man who had made the mistake of publicly insulting Jaja, were at the bottom of the sea. The owners of the *Cramoise* were advised that Jaja had risked the lives of his men to save their ship from the natives. Jaja and Nimba had strengthened their harbor and the *Cramoise* owners would soon pay them a handsome fee for 'protecting' their ship. The hapless members of Char's tribe had been sold by Jaja to both Captain Roux and to Captain Christopher who now had three hundred slaves crammed into the hold of the *Nelly*. Even Jaja could not recall ever conducting such a successful and treacherous series of trades. He and Nimba had betrayed every party involved in the scheme, killed or sold as slaves every human they contacted and were now to be rewarded as heroes by the rightful owners of the *Cramoise* for "saving" their ship. Praise be to the gods who smile upon murderers, kidnappers and thieves.

PRINCE of SAND - Chapter Four ... Le Passage du Milieu / The Middle Passage

I screamed once, and loudly. His cat-o-nine tails ripped into my left side. It felt like fire. My rib cage was on fire! Fuck! And what was my crime? The mistake of having made eye contact with this cold monster four days earlier when we had been shoved onto this ship from hell? Whipped again, I winced in pain but made no sound while staring down at my feet. He was behind me, out of my sight, but I knew who was whipping me. Then he was at my side, moving past me. Out of the corner of my left eye I saw the handle of his weapon. One distinctive strand of red cord was laced into the handle. If this whip was close by, I was certain to be struck. If I knew where he was on deck, I did all that I could to avoid him. I dreamed of killing the man gripping that red handle. I dreamed of killing the seaman called Billy Simms.

Earlier that same year, in the spring of 1760, young Simms had signed on to crew on his first slaver, the *Nelly*. Some of the men he had sailed with refused offers to crew on a slaver, fearful of the many dangers present in shipping human cargo. Stories circulating among Liverpool sailors made it clear – violence was common on these crowded vessels where captives, desperate to break out of their chains, might attack a member of the crew whenever given a chance. The ships were intentionally over crowded for the leg of the journey from Africa to the islands or South America, the so-called Middle Passage. Fevers and illness among the captives crammed below the deck killed some slaves but also struck down members of the crew. Yes, it was dangerous work and for that reason the pay was rich. Billy Simms could earn, for one ten month slave voyage, almost double what he would normally earn. But the money really made no difference to Simms. The dangers of a slaver were not foremost on his mind. For Billy, the good Captain Christopher was taking the *Nelly* to sea and that was all that really mattered.

Captain C had been busy the past six years sailing the *Abundance* from Liverpool to the European ports of call and on trade routes in the Mediterranean. The owners of the *Abundance* were well pleased with his efficient command of their ship and they certainly had the Captain in mind as they raised additional funds to bring the *Nelly* into their fleet. These Liverpool investors had been working on this plan with Captain Christopher for just over two years. The ship was commissioned out of one of the colonies in North America, Rhode Island. Native black oak lumber there was used primarily for the hulls of slave ships as it proved to be superior in resisting the warm water conditions of the African coast that would rot other hulls at an alarming rate. Once fitted and ready for sea, Captain C had watched with a quickened pulse as she was brought safely into Liverpool. Simms had never hesitated when offered a berth on the *Nelly*. Wherever Captain C was going, Simms planned to be at his side.

On board whatever ship that was under Captain C's command was the only time Billy had ever felt at home. Even after he met Janet, a strikingly handsome maid in a dirty tavern of Liverpool where the *Abundance* crew traded their pay for rum, he was always anxious to return to sea. Janet was a lot like Billy. Young and alone in a city that ignored them both, they were each remarkably attractive yet had no awareness as to how to socialize with the strangers that came into their lives. Janet shared a room in the home of an older couple near the tavern. Her roommate was a woman who served meals in another pub. When the *Abundance* was in port, Billy would sit in a corner of the tavern and stare at Janet as she worked. Janet brought him home one night and took him into her bed. After that night, Billy seldom slept anywhere else. The other woman moved out when Janet became pregnant. Billy and Janet Simms were two fifteen year old children now expecting a child of their own.

Three to six month voyages were common for Billy and the crew of the *Abundance*. It never made much of an impression on him that other people might be affected by his daily presence in their lives followed by an extended absence while he was at sea. Billy Simms was a sailor, first and last. Janet was drawn to him as they satisfied one another's physical cravings as two teenagers often do. Honestly, Billy's strong young body and his insistence that their room be kept scrubbed as clean as the deck of the *Abundance* brought a sense order to Janet. Her thick auburn hair with a rich red hue offset by her ample milk white breasts drew admiring attention from men and women alike. She was of medium height and thick in the hip. Janet was more attractive than most young women in Liverpool but lacked any social awareness to compliment her looks. She had been given work in a tavern and was happy to have decent food to eat. It made sense to her that Billy would regularly want her in his bed. Life was a bit less hectic when he was at sea and more intense when he returned. Now she was pregnant and Billy was leaving on a new ship, the *Nelly,* for a longer voyage that would take nine moths to a year to complete. Well, two of the women from the tavern assured her they would help when the baby was due and it all seemed natural enough. Billy Simms went to sea on a slaver while Janet Simms began to swell with child. So be it.

Captain Christopher organized the crew to load their cargo for the voyage to Annamaboe, the west African port where the first load of slaves would be crammed into the *Nelly.* This being the *Nelly's* maiden voyage under Captain C, there were many additional tasks to be completed. All preparations seemed to go smoothly enough. Simms paid particular attention to his duties in handling the sails and rigging. He found his assigned quarters in the bow, to be shared with two others, acceptable and worked quickly to load the cloth, tools and iron bars that were the trade items most valued by the slave brokers, along with strong rum and brandy. The one aspect that worried Simms as the *Nelly* was made ready for slaving was ship security. Blacksmiths in Rhode Island must have crawled all over the ship for days having forged the shackles, fitted chains to raise and lower the barricado, installed swivel guns and countless locks. The steel bars used to create some cages on the slave level just below the main deck were heavy and strong. Even Billy Simms was aware enough to understand. This ship was built to help a small group of sailors force a large group of men to submit against their will. As a sailor on the *Abundance,* it had been Simms' job to help keep her fit to sail the seas. As part of the crew of the *Nelly,* he would be working to help keep hundreds of humans imprisoned during the Middle Passage. The horrors, the misery and the opportunities for danger that defined a Middle Passage would become quite real soon enough.

Abdul-Barry and I remained chained at the ankle when we were stuffed below into the four and a half foot high slave level below the main deck. Stooped and cramped, we could turn our heads to see what was happening around us and we could read the fear in our own faces. Stunned mothers clung to crying children. Some men tried to act as if they could control some element of this mind crushing tragedy. Others hung their heads and just tried to stay away from the vomit. We watched naked humans climbing over others trying, often without success, to reach the tub and pail placed in the middle of our new prison before they lost control and took a piss or a shit. To a degree you controlled what you could see or hear. You squeezed your eyes shut. You reversed your hands and pressed the heels tight over your ears touching your fingers together behind your head. But the ungodly smell, no one escaped the smell. Cover your nose?

You were forced to breath and taste the filth in the air. No. No one escaped the smell. Fear has a different odor all its own. It was our fourth day at sea when the spirits of death began to crawl over men chained together in this corner of hell. Grown men who seemed strong and fit in the morning were dead and being dropped into the sea by sunset. I was more afraid than I can ever remember. I watched Death come among us to touch whomever he pleased. One man would begin to sweat terribly as a scalding fever overtook him. The unlucky victim would collapse in terrible pain grabbing his stomach as bulging eyes rolled in his head. Sharp stomach pains doubled men up like sticks as they screamed like children. While the fever and pain increased, the foul watery crap would begin to flow down their legs from their ass. Abdul-Barry and I squeezed together as one trying to move away from any of these dying men but there was nowhere to hide. We watched men drained of all fluid from their bodies simply die at the end of the day. The sharks trailing the ship tore into their flesh when a body hit the water. Later I would learn that white men named this death fever 'dysentery'. Never had I imagined such a violent sickness. None of us had any idea how to try and keep this death away from us. Fear of what we could not see or understand brought many to tears. One day

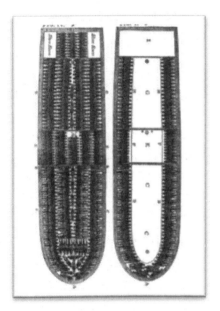

below that deck seemed like a month, one night a year. The days from a few weeks ago when we had been held captive back on the beach seemed like a holiday. The shattered memory of living free within sight of a mother's smile was pushed beyond my mind. The space that is left within has many names – pain, loneliness, despair. Living in this space a man learns to hate.

The crew was beginning to learn a routine for managing a slaver at sea. The tension always present between jailers and prisoners was suffocating over the first few days. Even Captain C was on edge as almost three hundred shackled natives, many all but naked, groaned in their filth below the deck. As the first week came to a close, many of the sailors were much more at ease in moving the slaves up onto deck for daily jumping and dance. The crew gained confidence in raising the barricado up for protection. The swivel guns were well placed. Strong men manning the guns swung them back and forth in front of frightened captives. Many slaves had never seen guns yet seemed to understand that they were to be feared. But all understood the whip. Every member of the crew had some type of whip or club in hand when slaves were brought up onto the deck. All but the smallest and the very weak felt the sting of the lash.

When the *Nelly* had first set sail from Liverpool, Captain C made no reference to the fact that slaves would be the cargo for the upcoming Middle Passage. It was business as usual for the first few weeks as the ship passed by the coast of Spain and Portugal bound for Africa. They were over one hundred miles down the African coast about four days out from Annamaboe when the captain steered the *Nelly* into a quiet cove along an uninhabited stretch of the coast and dropped anchor. For the next two days and nights the crew was drilled non-stop in moving men up and down from the slave deck. All security features were reviewed again and again. Swivel guns were loaded and fired by every member of the crew. Different members of the crew were shackled together at both ankle and neck and ordered to try and set themselves free. These drills helped each of the crew better understand the slaver but it also taught them that handling a human cargo would be different – and more dangerous – than any task they had ever experienced aboard any ship. The crates filled with whips and clubs had been opened on deck and each crew member selected one. Billy Simms had his eye on a cat-o-nine tails with a red strand in the handle. From that day forward, that whip was seldom out of his sight. In the midday heat on the second day, Olson, the helmsman, gathered the crew on the deck and spoke of the challenges ahead. He asked who on the crew had ever worked on a slaver. Craig, an older hand who had signed on for the last *Abundance* voyage, spoke up,

"Aye. I sailed on the *Cramoise* last year. We carried three hundred from the Gold Coast to Rio."

Olson asked, "And what do ye be sayin' bout a slaver?"

Craig looked at Olson, "I be sayin' the black bastards below this deck will stink and cry like nothin' a man can stand. Use your whip – flog everything that moves!"

Simms was clenching the handle of his whip so hard the leather left prints on his palm. "Everything that moves", the words seemed etched in his brain. If prisoners on the *Nelly* presented a threat to Captain C and crew, they would have to deal with Billy Simms. Others might hold back and whip or club only those that seemed to be making trouble but Simms would be a man to be reckoned with. In his mind he could see the first load of slaves coming on board. "Look at me", he thought. "I dare you, you black fucks. Look at me and learn to bend your head to Billy Simms!" Some of the sailors turned and stared as Simms lashed at the side of the mast.

Captain Christopher had been warned. As they anchored just off of Annamaboe in the middle of August, he realized that it would probably be mid-October at the earliest before he could expect to be outward bound for the island of Saint-Domingue. This slave trader he was dealing with, Jaja, had a reputation for being ruthless but also for being the one broker who could deliver strong young slaves quickly in large numbers. Thirty slaves had been delivered in the last week of August. Jaja had actually been rowed out to the Nelly explaining that he wanted to be sure that Captain C was pleased with the first group delivered. In fact, Jaja often tried to get aboard the ships he would be filling with slaves. How many guns were on board and what did the crew look like? Did the captain seem to have control of his crew? Jaja had learned long ago, the little things you could learn about another trader just might end up being a big thing. The little things you might reveal could end up killing you. Jaja always wanted to visit the ships. Actually, the dealings between Jaja and Christopher were productive for both men. Jaja had approached Captain C and whispered that an unusually large load of strong slaves could be coming available within a matter of days. This group was reported to be so big that the remainder of his ship would be filled in a single day. Would the captain of the *Nelly* be interested? It would be necessary for the ship receiving this delivery to be prepared to go to sea immediately given that an entire tribe was being brought out. There was always the possibility that some locals could become angry if a large number of their own were being kidnapped at one time. Any such ship that remained at anchor could draw their attention and anger. Jaja was not particularly concerned with maintaining order. He had more than enough muscle to brutally disperse unorganized locals who challenged his trade. It was simply an unnecessary risk. Nothing dispersed a crowd more completely and calmly than watching the three masts of the departing slaver disappear over the western horizon.

Captain Christopher was most certainly interested. Filling the *Nelly* so quickly would help greatly for two important reasons. First, the obvious benefit of gaining at least one full month in his schedule attracts the attention of any captain. More importantly, reducing the time that his ship would sit at anchor with strong angry slaves festering in the hold would be a comfort. But Captain C was not one to make a knee-jerk decision. He and Jaja talked through the details. Would the provisions still needed before weighing anchor be available on a priority basis from Jaja's suppliers? Their water supply would need to be freshened. Normally, Captain Christopher would prefer to be shipping slaves to the closest markets in South America but his investors had made arrangements for this first load from the *Nelly* to be unloaded in Saint-Domingue. This island destination extended his Middle Voyage by at least one full week. Jaja provided his assurance that every resource available would be focused on fitting out the *Nelly*. Both men wanted to see this ship safely bound for the islands. The commotion created when the slaves were first loaded onto the doomed *Cramoise* and just as quickly pulled off was hardly noticed by the crew of the *Nelly*. Heads had turned when some shots had been fired but the officers kept their men on task. Over two hundred and fifty incoming slaves were being rowed across the harbor. Every man was scrambling to have every task completed in order to store the heathens safely below and have the *Nelly* underway on her westward leg. Even the tension of taking on so many slaves could not dampen the excitement of going back to sea. Billy Simms and many just like him would go to their graves anxiously waiting to set sail for the next port of call.

Just as he had imagined, the boats rowing up to the ship were full of black men and a few women and Billy Simms was ready to introduce them to the *Nelly*. Frightened men stumbled forward as they tried to get their footing on the unfamiliar deck. Naked women huddled close to one another. Foul smelling sailors shouted orders that the slaves could not begin to understand. Simms pushed slaves along toward the opening that led them down to their dismal space. His eyes nervously searched back and forth between prisoners as he tried to find one to return his stare. The man who looked up and first held his gaze would soon be filled with regret.

The first week at sea had passed without major incidence. The captain anticipated making Saint-Domingue by the first week of November. Another five weeks or so and the *Nelly's* crew would have their maiden Middle Passage behind them. Captain C dared hope they might sell all of their slaves, trade for a valuable cargo of sugar and coffee and be back in Liverpool by February of the new year. The trust placed in him by his partners and the confidence of the crew would grow accordingly if all were back safe home in Liverpool early in 1761. But first, moving these slaves safely to Saint-Domingue would require their full attention.

Once the *Nelly* was back at sea, all orders came from Captain Christopher. Yes, the rules that governed international sea going vessels were well established and certain laws prevailed, but the captain of the ship shouldered tremendous responsibility and with that came unchallenged authority once at sea. Regarding the treatment of human cargo, different captains gave rein to different levels of mischief. This was a new situation for Captain C and his instinct was to trust in his crew. All felt the pressure of completing this first trade for slaves as quickly as possible. Officers were free to assign any slaves they chose to tend to their quarters. For the crew, the number of slaves assigned to their cramped berths would be closely monitored. Once in Saint-Domingue, every slave would need to be sold for the highest price possible. Bruised and battered slaves would not bring a good price. The rules on the *Nelly* were basic – you could do what you wanted with a slave as long as you did not damage the product prior to sale.

Billy Simms and his two mates, sharing a small space in the bow, pulled two healthy teenage girls from the filthy slave cages and locked them in their berth. The girls were not shackled to one another and the comfort of the modest bunks was theirs to claim when they were left alone. At first, the girls felt lucky to be out of the terrible filth of the common space and placed in their own private cell. They were terrified of these men but at least they had each other to cling to. The three sailors were on different shifts and seldom were two men there at the same time. Simms made one thing quite clear to these girls – the deck of this small space was to be kept scrubbed as clean as any surface on the entire ship. The other requirements of the two held captive varied based on the appetites of the man who happened to be in the berth at any given time. Two girls, three men and no rules beyond a prohibition on open sores and obvious scars. Billy Simms completed his watch and entered his quarters. The two young girls huddled in a corner, arms about one another. Simms saw the fear in their eyes as he scanned the floor that was freshly scrubbed. All was in order as he squeezed the grip of his whip.

The darkness surrounding us below decks could not hide the despair of hundreds now sailing away from shores they would never lay eyes on again. Abdul-Barry explained why the ship was sailing west;

"Sugar. White men have land across this water. On the land they grow the sugarcane. Many slaves are needed to gather the sugarcane. They crush the cane, make the sugar and trade it to be sold where the white men live. The sugar is like gold to the captains of these ships. We are the slaves they will trade for the sugar. They gather us from traders such as Jaja, we are shipped across this water to be sold as sugarcane slaves."

Everything about this nightmare was new to me. My mind said I was still a young hunter cared for by his mother. There were moments when my mother, Sanja, was so close I could smell the herbs she wore in her hair. I would turn my face to hers as she came up behind me and reached up, placing her hand on my shoulder, squeezing it gently;

"Yamar, each night you have been working with your spears and hides long after dark. It is time for you to put such work aside and sleep. Go inside your hut. I will sit by the entrance and keep all others away while you rest. Rest, my son, you must now take rest."

My eyes would feel so heavy and the bedroll on the floor of my hut was clean and comfortable. "Sanja, you are right. But I cannot find the entrance to my hut. The captain of this ship has told his men to push me down this hole. I am beaten with the whip when I move toward my hut."

"Ship? Yamar, come away from this 'ship' that you speak of and I will lead you to your hut. Now, Yamar, follow me now and take your rest."

And I would begin to follow Sanja as she turned and walked forward into a dark mist. Each time I tried to follow, I would lose sight of her, yet I could still clearly hear her calm instructions. In a low voice, I always called to her,

"Sanja, go slower so I can see you. Where have you gone?"

"Here, Yamar, I am right here. Come toward me now and rest inside your hut."

Always, as I stepped toward her voice, there would be some kind of door facing me that I did not recognize. The door had no handle and layers of thin bark covered the door. I would begin to peel away the bark but there was always another layer in my way. Just as some large sections of bark seemed to fall away, the sharp sting of a whip on my back had me screaming in pain and I snapped my head around to face my enemy. The nightmare always ended at this moment and I would suffer the depression of realizing that my mother was nowhere near. The face of the man whipping me from behind was always a blur. By the time I could turn around, no one was in sight and I was back in the reality of my miserable prison. It did not matter that I never clearly saw the face of the man holding the whip. Billy Simms and I both knew who was gripping the handle of that whip.

Abdul-Barry said that he had heard members of the crew talk about the island of Saint-Domingue. He told me that a place called 'South America' was closer and most white captains sailed their ships to this 'South America'. But some islands further west, like this Saint-Domingue, also had the sugarcane and ships could sell their slaves when they stopped at these islands. It was difficult for me to picture the places that Abdul-Barry tried to describe. I was sad to think that we were not going to stop at the closest place. I could not imagine where we were going but I desperately wanted to get away from this ship and away from the big water. I asked Abdul-Barry;

"When do you think we will get to this new place? How long must we stay in this hole? I do not know if I can live through any more nights in this place. The death spirit climbs over us every night and I can feel how close he is to taking me with him."

I could not know just how long this Middle Passage would continue. If it did not end soon, many more chained below the deck would be fed to the sharks. It was early in November and we began to receive some extra food. The amount of time that we were left up on the deck in fresh air was longer. Fair weather made the time on deck a welcome break from the terror below. It was late one afternoon when male slaves were lined up in groups between the masts. Buckets of palm oil were placed on the deck. We were ordered to rub our shoulders, arms and legs with the oil. I began to understand. With more food and fresh water, I sensed that I might survive. Abdul-Barry supported the hope that we might soon be off the ship. I crouched next to the forward mast and squinted toward the sun, now large and low above the light blue water. How many times had I been bought and sold since that moment when a net fell on my head and I became a piece of property owned by another man? The sound of the boar grunting in a rage as he tore Malek apart was around me. The colors of the sun and sea were brilliant. Strangely, I found myself wondering how Malek would feel if he were still alive and chained to me on this deck. Had men from our village found Malek's bones? Soon I was to be sold once again and it somehow seemed familiar.

Another night had passed. It was very early. The sea seemed completely still, the surface as smooth as glass. Slaves around me still groaned in their pain but there was a murmur moving through the group. Birds were working above and it was said that land could be seen from the deck. Soon we were brought up onto the deck. This was not part of the normal routine, to be up on deck in the morning, and signaled that some change could be taking place. Again, the buckets of oil were placed among us. The barricado was pulled up and, as always, men moved the swivel guns back and forth, but now everyone seemed full of energy. Off to my right, from the corner of my eye, I sensed the presence of my tormentor. Billy Simms, whip in hand, stood guard with other sailors closely watching our group. But their officers were also gathered and there was little clubbing or whipping taking place. We all began to turn our heads from side-to-side, much more aware of the sea and where the ship was moving. Now we could begin to see masts from other ships! Regardless of what might come next, it seemed this Middle Passage was coming to an end. Abdul-Barry said he felt certain that the land we could now see was the island of Saint-Domingue. We drew closer to the shore and turned to the southwest with the shore now passing by on our right. For hours we sailed along the length of the island before bearing north. The ship then came about heading back east as we entered a large protected harbor. Some sailors had actually gone below with mops and buckets filled with strong smelling liquid that was sloshed about in the filth that had been our disgusting prison for many weeks. This space could never be made acceptable for humans but clearly there was an effort being made to make the *Nelly* seem less terrible. I was excited and actually felt hopeful. I had not felt this way for what seemed like a very long time. Breathing quickly, I mumbled to Abdul-Barry,

"Abdul-Barry, do you think we will be taken off this ship today? Oh Vordun, please let it be so. Have we truly survived this trip to hell?"

His response made sense, "We will leave this ship but it will be tomorrow, not today. No one will be allowed to die now. Each slave now alive on this ship will bring gold coins to the captain. I think they will want to trade us for their prize as soon as they can get us off the ship in the morning."

We received better food and rubbed ourselves with oil before being returned below deck. As terrible as these nights had become, at least now the end seemed in sight. We were moving forward toward a bench when I heard my name called,

"Prince, who will come for us now? Is your father, Kalem, bringing hunters to find us and to take us home? Prince, take me back with you. Take me, take me home."

It was growing dark and I squinted trying to see those around me. The voice was not familiar. Who could possibly be calling for me, a prisoner in this hole, to take them back across the big water? Who was asking for my father to save them? Two small older men were curled up on a shelf to my left. They were hunched over and appeared quite frail. Their backs were up against the side of the hull. One thin arm reached out and a trembling hand reached for my elbow. I leaned over, our noses almost touching, and stared into vacant eyes. Who is this old man? Instinctively I was pulling back when the eyes registered with my brain. Batou!

I was stunned, "Batou? Batou, is that you? Oh Batou, have you been given any food today?"

"Take me, Prince. Take me home. Is your father coming? Prince, when can we go home?" The skin draped over bones was a shell of Batou. His feeble voice kept mumbling about going home. His hair was now half grey and half black. It was difficult to believe that one person could lose so much of their body just over the weeks of the Middle Passage. The movement of other slaves shuffled us forward. Abdul-Barry spotted a place to sit further up the deck so we pushed forward and onto the bench.

"That man you call Batou, he is broken. I have seen such men and many women after they have been taken prisoner and lost their hope. They cannot understand what is around them. He will leave this ship but he will quickly die" was Abdul-Barry's observation.

Yes, Batou's end was upon him. I had just stared into his death mask. The spirit of death would remain close to me on this island, close to all in the sugarcane.

PRINCE of SAND - Chapter Five ... Deplacement des esclaves et deplacement du sucre /Moving Slaves and Moving Sugar

The *Nelly* was not long in Port Au Prince. The sale of the slaves had brought the kind of price that Captain Christopher's partners had planned for. All hands were happy to now trade a human cargo for a full load of sugar and coffee with the sacks stacked in row after row filling what had been a staggering scene of suffering. With a full crew of twenty-one fit and ready for the third and final leg of their ten month trade mission, Captain C was genuinely pleased and, perhaps, a bit proud. The responsibility for over three hundred men and women from Annamaboe to Port Au Prince had worn on the captain. It was something he had planned for so the tension had been expected, but a man cannot know the toll until he has been in the harness. Slaves had died onboard the *Nelly*. Moving slaves across the Atlantic on thin rations with fever and dysentery following, no ship could move such numbers without losing some of the cargo. But to make it through with your crew in sound condition was an accomplishment of note. So Captain C was particularly disappointed to learn, when the men returned to ship after liberty the third night in port, that the *Nelly* would make the last leg home with only twenty hands as her crew.

Port Au Prince was a new shipping and trade center compared to the established ports of Europe and the Mediterranean. By 1761, the French authorities ruling Saint-Domingue were increasingly impressed and committed to the money that was being made from sugar. It seemed that traders would pay dearly for all the sugar the plantations could supply. The number of ships that now crowded the harbors such as Port Au Prince had grown faster than anyone expected. The loosely controlled docks were crammed with Spanish, Portuguese, British, and Dutch traders joining the French. Sailors from these countries were mixed with deck hands from South America, the French Creole natives from Saint-Domingue and other nearby islands and a growing number of men from the colonies in North America. Layered into this bold mix were the Africans who were now shipped in as slaves in huge numbers so that huge amounts of sugar could be shipped out. Moving slaves in so sugar could be moved out, it was as simple as that. When crew members reached Port Au Prince after a Middle Passage was completed and could move their prisoners off ship, their collective relief was tremendous. The crew of the *Nelly* was no different. Perhaps they were feeling even bigger about themselves given that these slaves, now profitably sold into the plantations of Saint-Domingue, had been their first as slavers. Billy Simms and his mates drew some of their back pay in gold coin and, in small groups with wide grins, they scattered among the debauched taverns and gambling houses crammed around the harbor.

"Simms, hold up your bloody arse and wait for me before I rip that pecker of yours from between thee balls and feed it to the fuckin' gulls!" It seemed that Anderson, the cook, and Billy always ended up in a group together. Billy grinned as he looked back over his shoulder and waved for the foulest mouth cook on the seven seas to hurry up and join them. Jones and Jackson were about. Simms had earned their trust as one who pulled his weight onboard and who would not hesitate to throw himself at any man who threatened a member of Captain C's crew. Men take the measure of each other. This crew had watched Simms grow up quickly as a young man who cared for nothing but his ship and they understood that Billy Simms carried with him a passionate loyalty to Captain Christopher. It was not something anyone gave much thought to. If Simms' everything was the *Nelly*, that was his business. But it did count for something if danger was ever about. In the back of their heads, they knew that Simms would stop at nothing to bring injury to any man who might do them harm – any man. Simms had no fear of anyone who challenged one of the *Nelly's* crew. The idea of fear never even crossed his mind. When you have nothing to lose, you play by rules others may fail to understand.

The men had taken their fill of rum and ale. In a scene played out countless times in ports around the world, this group had roamed up and down the docks reveling in a rare break from their responsibilities when under sail. On this night, their experiences having just moved slaves across the Atlantic gave rise to new stories. Sailors and soldiers trade such stories among themselves when the rum is flowing. Not the false bravado of boys hoping to impress their peers, these men were sharing private experiences that would never be repeated around their officers. Privacy was an unknown commodity aboard ship so secrets were few but the crew of the *Nelly* was curious. Men were not accustomed to having women onboard. Now, women had not only been onboard but the Captain had made it clear – over the many weeks of the Middle Passage, the crew could take ownership of these slaves as long as the goods were returned in decent shape. So who did what to whom and what were the reactions from these men who all took advantage of the situation?

"The little bitch was a crawlin' and tryin' to hide every time I be throwin' back the hatch", roared Jackson as he poured down half a tankard of ale, some of which actually made it into his mouth. Billy's eyes gleamed as he grinned and nodded to himself. The stories were predictable. One seemed to basically be the continuation of another. "The first one cried so long and hard, she was doing nothin' but moaning and blowin' snot. Dragged her ass back down into the hole and pulled me out another, I did. T'was a good trade for ol' Tom, I'll tell you that!" Men laughed and slapped each other across their shoulders. "What about you, Sir William Simms? Did them two wenches in your bunk trim your sails, lad? Well, did they now?"

Billy laughed along with the others. No stories were coming from Simms. It was not his style and no one cared. As the shouts and laughter rolled around the table, Simms was lost in his own thoughts. The Middle Passage was over but the *Nelly* was a slaver and the Middle Passage would be repeated as often as Captain C took the crew back to Africa. About every year, as far as Billy could figure, some young slave girls would be herded onto the *Nelly*. For a stretch of weeks, year after year, Billy Simms could own slave girls while on the *Nelly* and lock them in his berth. All of this would be his at no cost to Simms while he was drawing slaver wages. Captain C was a good man to follow. For a stretch of weeks, year after year, Billy Simms would move his slave girls with his whip. God he loved that whip.

Now the rum houses were starting to empty out as sailors stumbled back toward their ships. Others had more on their mind. Women working through the night when ships crowded into Port Au Prince were taking risks. Some had no choice as they were forced to mingle with drunks as long as the tavern owners kept their doors open for business. Others were part of another plan. The men who stay late are often the men who can be easily separated from their gold. If done with skill, the target may not even be aware that he has been fleeced until the next day back on the ship. Hard women living a hard life look for easy money. The play was not complicated and had been practiced for hundreds of years. Find one or two hangers-on who were soaked in rum and practice the brazen blunt seduction that labels a woman as a whore. Move the man into dark corners. Encourage his advances and pretend to find his stink attractive. Allow him to paw breasts and hips. Touch him in ways that convince him he is in charge. Beg him to take you to your special place. Once out and on the dark streets and alleys that twist among the warehouses and shops, the sailor would be on unfamiliar ground.

The shipmate named Clarke had been under the control of rum since the age of twelve. He was basically a loner on his new ship, the *Nelly*, and he had taken on all the rum the barkeep would send his way. Billy had hung around as well sensing that something more might be in store this night. The barmaid wearing a tight and open blouse was rubbing up against Clarke and pouring rum down his open throat. She had hair as black as coal. Her dark features fit her tan complexion. Clarke was her mark. She had him laughing as she lifted coins from his pockets, enough to pay twice the cost of the rum. She pulled him toward her. They were up and out the front door walking into the dark of the night. Billy had been over at a side table, alone and watching this whore cover Clarke as he took more and more rum. They were both drunk but, after gulping enough to make him numb, Billy Simms did not seem to care much one way or another about drinking any more. Billy just wanted to be with his mates from the *Nelly*. If most of the men were returning to ship, he was usually leaving with them. If one or two were going whoring, well, he might be persuaded to stay. Tonight, this bitch had caught his attention as she allowed Clarke to put his hands up her crimson skirts. She showed no fear and laughed as things got a little rough. Billy slipped out the door behind them and began to follow. Stepping out of the cramped tavern and into the night air cleared his head slightly. He squinted to keep them in sight moving down toward the wharf to his right. There was a creek that emptied into the harbor up ahead. The alley turned sharply to the right and ran back up along the side of the creek. Clarke was leaning on the barmaid as she led him up the alley close to the small huts that were lined up along the left side of the street, squeezed between the sandy gravel and the creek. Suddenly she pulled him to the left up onto the stoop of a tiny shack. The frame of the door and the single window of this whitewashed structure under a tin roof had been painted a bright aqua blue. Clarke followed the woman through the open door into the single room under that roof. She used her foot to shut the door behind her as the two stumbled forward. Billy could hear Clarke laugh. He listened and thought about what was coming. It would be simple. Billy Simms would walk quietly into the room and watch Clarke having his way with the whore. It would not matter to Billy if Clarke liked it or not. Besides, Clarke was so drunk he would remember little from this night. And it sure as hell didn't matter if the bitch liked it or not. For Billy, it would be more fun if she got mad. After weeks at sea with frightened slaves, slapping this bitch around the room would be a nice change of pace.

Everything had gone quiet. Billy listened closely for what seemed like a long time. The creek, so close that it almost came up into the shack, was running full on the high tide. There was a stirring inside. Someone walked across the floor. Billy reached out and pushed the door open trying to see inside. He stepped in and was surprised to see three people clustered together against the far wall. Clarke was stretched out on a cot and seemed to be asleep or passed out. The woman, standing over him, was holding Clarke's britches. And there was a man kneeling between Clarke and the backdoor, a man Billy had never seen before. He appeared to be tying Clarke's wrists to the cot. The woman, clearly surprised, turned and stared at Simms. The man was small, about Billy's size, and dark. Once he saw Billy, he slid his arms up under Clarke's shoulders pulling him off the cot and out the back onto the few boards nailed to posts that were sunk in the mud. Now the woman dropped the pants and came toward Billy. She shoved him in the chest telling him to get out. Something snapped and Simms did not hesitate. The woman's feet never touched the floor as Billy exploded forward. In three large steps they were both through the rear door, out onto the boards and the woman was sailing backward into the creek. Billy's legs were tangled with Clarke and the stranger. He stepped back into the doorway and saw a flash of steel from his left. Clarke was unconscious and lying flat on his back just outside the backdoor. Now the man held a knife to Clarke's throat, grabbing him by the hair with his left hand, and barked orders to Billy in some language he could not understand. The only thing on the flimsy dock was an old oar leaning against the shack. Billy grabbed the oar and, raising it over his head, turned to his left to face the man. Simms would never forget what happened next. The image of the knife being drawn across Clarke's throat was frozen in his brain. The man never took his narrowed eyes from Billy and seemed to grin slightly as he moved the knife. In a blink, Clarke's throat was laid open as a grunting noise bubbled up and out from the opening now gushing hot blood. The killer dropped Clarke's head and rose, the knife in his right hand now covered with blood. Billy swung the oar, slamming the man in his left shoulder. As he moved to deflect the blow with his left forearm, the man dropped his arm over the oar blade and tried to pin it against his side so he could thrust the knife with his right. Before the man could attack, Billy shifted his weight onto his right leg, moved both his hands slightly toward the middle of the oar, pulled the blade back toward himself with his right and snapped the handle forward toward his attacker with his left. He used all the strength and leverage he could deliver. Instinctively pulling his head back, the man was caught flush on the right temple by the oar handle and his knees buckled. Billy never thought about the knife, he never remembered seeing the woman and all he knew about Clarke was that his blood was all over the dock. He brought the oar over his head, slammed it down and crushed open the man's skull. Simms continued to club the man until he was satisfied that he was more than dead. Dropping the oar, he never looked back as he stepped through the shack and out into the alley.

By morning Billy's blood-splattered shirt and a couple of bricks had been slipped into a sack that went to the bottom of the harbor. Port Au Prince officials made some inquiries after it was determined that the *Nelly* had a member of her crew who was unaccounted for. Captain Christopher viewed the body and confirmed that Clarke was from his ship. There was little that could be done. It seemed no one could identify the small man with his face beaten in. One sailor and some drifter were both dead down around the roughest part of the docks. It would not be the last time Port Au Prince would begin its day with such news. The barmaid had pulled herself up and out of the creek. She was just happy to be alive and would keep her mouth shut. Clarke was dead, Billy Simms had destroyed his killer and the *Nelly* would set sail for Liverpool under twenty hands. You were alive, you moved on.

Try as he might, Captain Christopher could never remove the stench from the *Nelly's* holding area below the deck where thousands of prisoners would travel from freedom to slavery. Barrels of turpentine, bags of lyme, hours of scrubbing – still, you would always know the *Nelly* was a slaver. Prince was not around two days later to watch her sail from the harbor on the rising tide. She lay heavy under a full load. The sugar and coffee brought huge profits to her owners, ten months of pay for her crew and an attractive bonus to Captain C and his officers. Money was available to refit the ship, to add more locks and move guns to the most effective spots thus increasing her capacity to move more slaves. Prince had no need to ever lay eyes on the *Nelly* again. The arc of his life was forever altered and there would be no path home. Never was that more evident than earlier that week when he, Abdul-Barry and hundreds of others were sold to the plantation owners of Saint-Domingue.

Abdul-Barry spoke about what was coming next,

"Now that we are off the ship the change of ownership will come quickly. The captain is done with us, ready to be rid of us. Buyers will want to get us loaded up and into their fields as quickly as they can."

Prince grew weary just thinking of being sold yet again. Of course, never having been owned by a planter and enslaved on a plantation, he had given no thought to the possibility that this might be the final time he would be sold. It had not occurred to him that he might spend the remainder of his life working himself to death for the next man who placed a chain around his neck. How would all of these slaves be sold? Who would decide which of them were to be sold first? Where would they be taken? His relief at being back on land and off of the wretched ship was quickly giving way to the weight of what stood before him.

The market, just two blocks from the docks, was a simple structure. The open-air facility was fifty feet wide and stretched out one hundred fifty feet in length. Every twenty five feet there were brick columns erected about ten feet in height. So there were a dozen squares of open space, six bays side-by-side, all covered by the low hanging roof that sloped to either side. The seven pillars running down the middle were taller, about twelve feet in height, creating pitch in the roof. The roof stretched out beyond the pillars by a good four feet all around the market creating an overhang and providing much needed shade in the tropical conditions. Large canopies were rolled up and lashed to cross beams running from pillar to pillar on the perimeter of the low-slung structure. If severe weather blew in, the canopies could be unfurled and tied down providing a measure of protection for those within. On average days, different locals would sell their wares from one of the bays – the fishermen's catch, local crops, leather goods or the display by a local tinker. But on days when a slaver unloaded, the bays between the mustard colored brick pillars were cleared out. The local slave auctioneers made their arrangements with the ship's captain and the process unfolded at a brisk pace. Normally, the auctioneer separated the goods down the middle of the structure. The most fit and highly valued males would be stood on platforms running between the middle pillars and told to face out toward the perimeter. Often, canopies were lowered behind them dividing the market down the middle with the highly valued males traded on one side while the others were collected and presented on the opposite side of the market. Buyers had access under the roof and were encouraged to inspect the prisoners. Once the auction began, efforts were made to move the process along and complete the sales without delay.

We had been collected up on deck and rubbed down with oil. Members of the crew had watched us closely as we were marched off the ship. It was late in the morning and unseasonably warm for November. I kept my eyes down but constantly moved them from right to left and back again fearful that the one who so often abused me, the hated one they called Billy Simms, would appear at my side, whip in hand. But there was no flogging or whipping now that the time for sale was at hand. Simms never came into view. Men working with the auctioneer separated us into two groups as we were herded up the street toward the market. Locals lined the street. We were a curiosity but drew only minimal attention. The arrival of black men and a few women being moved from a ship to the slave market was part of the Port Au Prince routine. There was more interest in the fact that buyers from the plantations were gathered in town. These men brought money to trade and the smell of gold was on the streets. It seemed everyone, from the small barefoot boys dancing on the corner for coins, to the well dressed shop owners were out in front of the slave buyers working for their attention. Ports of call everywhere seemed to share this second wind for commerce when larger vessels arrived safely and delivered cargo of significant value. The town normally moved at its own pace subject to the tide and the routine activity of smaller boats coming and going in a slower tropical climate. You might see vacant storefronts, fishermen moonlighting as painters or carpenters, two or three women running a tavern – the normal level of activity seemed to function with a group of relatively few locals handling the commerce. But when the tall three masts of the trade ships rounded the southwest point and came into the harbor, the town seemed to draw breath, rise up on its hindquarters and throw off its complacency. Certain shop windows, normally dark and empty, seemed full of goods for sale and were definitely open for business. The small run-down tavern that was operated by two old women with seldom more than a handful of customers would be almost full with fresh-faced younger women gathered at the front door calling in men off the street. They now referred to every white man in town as "sailor boy" and it was clear that more than rum and chowder was being offered for sale. Everybody was out to grab some of the gold coins that had come into town when the black slaves were about to be sold. Property was about to change hands – let the buyer beware.

The pace had quickened as we were hurried into the market. Abdul-Barry and I were separated from each other as each slave now stood alone with our wrists and our ankles secured by shackles. There were a few buyers who were being brought past

us before the auction process began. The traders called this the "scramble". It seems that the larger buyers from select plantations were invited to quickly review the product and make their selections at predetermined prices before others were allowed to bid. Make no mistake, traders moving slaves through the market were not concerned with treating all potential buyers as equals. The reality was that a large plantation owner was always selling sugar. Therefore, that same owner was always buying slaves. The men who always needed eight or ten new bodies to replace the men and women that had been worked to their deaths deserved preferential treatment. These good customers knew what they were looking for in a productive slave and they would not hesitate to pay a fair price for quality product. It was good business to encourage this group of customers to step up and make their selections. Rapidly now some of the slaves around me, standing in front of the canopy dividing the two sides of the market, were being pointed out by some well dressed buyers and just as quickly being led away. It seemed as soon as we understood that we were being led into the market, the strongest young men among us were being moved out.

I hardly had time to mumble some words of good-bye to Abdul-Barry. He was one of the first to be selected and was quickly taken away from the display area. Some of the buyers taking part in this scramble eyed me as they moved among us. Sweat was thick on my forehead and on my upper lip. You know you are being watched. You can feel their eyes on you and you imagine the conversation they are probably having with themselves;

"That one looks good, but will he survive the first summer in the 'cane? I cannot afford to have them going to an early grave. Five is my number - I'll need at least five good years from each to get my money back out of them."

And then, in a moment, I was prodded with the end of a cane and, as the man on the other end raised his head toward the auctioneer, I became the property of yet another new master. The handlers for this buyer herded six of us just outside of the market where a large cart was harnessed behind two mules. We would wait, chained to the cart, until the buyer had completed his business. I watched the four members of a family from the tribe of Mandinka. They had been fellow prisoners on the *Nelly*. The father stood tall while the mother and two children huddled next to him in the trading area. The father was a tremendous individual, clearly the most remarkable physical specimen being displayed for sale. He held his head high, his jaw clenched with eyes looking forward as if gazing at a distant horizon. His forearms made normal shackles look like tiny bracelets that could not fit around him. Handlers had to wrap a heavy chain about his wrists and fasten a lock through the links leaving about a six-inch length of the chain hanging below his enormous hands. Once you saw this warrior, it was hard to look away from him. Shoulders as wide as his wife's outstretched arms sloped down from a neck as thick as most men's thigh. The strength in his chest rivaled that of the most splendid animal. The tight lines rippling across his stomach led to a waist that seemed remarkably small given all that it supported. This man stood on two legs of such strength that it was hard to imagine what might move him. His wife, a strong woman of better than normal stature, came to just below his chest when she stood next to him. The mother and her children appeared out of place standing on the same platform as the most fit young men but it made sense to me that this family would be sold together.

Buyers had crowded around this giant and bid his price to more than twice that of any other slave. The woman stood just to the right of him trying to be calm but her fear could not be masked. The children, a boy and a girl, were each around nine or ten years of age. They stood on either side and slightly behind their mother. Sensing her mother's fear, the girl cried softly while hiding her face on the woman's thigh. Something like a cheer rose from the group as the highest bid was called by the auctioneer. Men leaned on one another, rising on their toes in an effort to identify the successful bidder. In the same motion, they turned their faces to gaze one more time upon this most impressive of men, many now nodding slightly as if they too would have traded so many gold coins in order to claim such a property as their own. The heavy sweet odor of tobacco and brandy blended with the pungent sweat of both buyers and those being offered up for sale. The resulting aroma was something that hard men were drawn to. Horse races, cock fights, hangings and slave auctions – all of these were popular diversions for locals in Port Au Prince.

The group was unwinding. There were other sales to be made. Quickly, the handlers had moved the family down from the display stand. But the buyer had an urgent message to be whispered to the auctioneer. Now the woman and two children were led further to the right of the father whose expression remained unmoved. It became clear that only the warrior had been purchased and the owner would be leaving immediately with his new slave. The woman and her two young ones were still for sale. As the wife began to absorb the cruelty of her fate, she wore the look of someone who had just witnessed death. Low and long, the moan that rolled out from her left me chilled and feeling empty yet few of those around me seemed to notice. Clearly, the spirit of a slave woman being crushed at auction was old news in Port Au Prince. Nobody cared. As her knees buckled, handlers were trying to force the warrior out of the market but he set his feet and thus remained in place. He paid no attention to their grabbing his arms. As they pulled on him, he fixed his stare on the boy. Slowly, the son shifted from behind his mother and, lending her his support, made certain that she would not fall. He then raised his head, returning his father's gaze, but no words passed between them. Strange, but it now seemed the boy was a few inches taller and appeared to be older than his little sister. Only when he was ready did the warrior allow himself to be moved toward the wagon that would carry him out of Port Au Prince. The buyer had brought a sturdy cage, well secured to the bed of the wagon, and his new slave was quietly loaded. Some local boys ran alongside as the two horses under harness began to pull the wagon out of town.

Looking back at the woman, it seemed that another animated discussion with the auctioneer was stirring a few of the men around her and the two children. One of the buyers had very directly reached over to grab the woman by her arm. He proceeded to pull away the ragged cloth tied by a cord around her waste. Her head was then tilted back by his hand on her chin and he pushed back her upper lip to inspect her teeth and gums. Another shopper squeezed one of her breasts. Satisfied, the first buyer raised four fingers indicating a price and, in a direct comment to the auctioneer, apparently stated that the woman was the only slave he would purchase. Her children were of no interest to him.

Now another owner had asserted himself and he spoke directly to the potential buyer;

"Bon dieu home, au nom de notre seigneur Jesus-Christ ... Good god man, in the name of our lord, Jesus Christ, should you purchase the mother, you purchase the two children! It is the Christian thing to do!"

The conversation was dragging on. It seemed the potential buyer was losing interest. I was loaded up into the cart with five others. Within an hour, we would be well out of Port Au Prince on a road heading north/northeast away from the harbor toward the huge sugar plantation operated by the Royer family. I never knew which plantation the huge warrior was sent to and I have no idea what became of the woman and her children.

It now struck me that I had not seen Batou all morning. Desperately I wrenched my head around looking back toward the market. It was pointless as we were already well away from the auction and I could no longer recognize individuals from such a distance. I would never see Batou or any others from my tribe ever again. Suddenly, my mind was taken back to that dawn four months earlier when we were hunting wild boars. The boar was goring Malek and then Malek was dead. Batou and I, along with the others, had become prisoners. The only member of our group who turned and ran, Ganja, was probably now enjoying warm nights in his comfortable hut. Batou and I had been bought and sold at least six or seven times. Batou was alone and on his own wearing a death mask that would allow him but little time. I was alone and on my own. No one could tell how long I might survive.

As the cart bumped along on that hot and dusty afternoon, I found myself thinking of the man who had squealed about "our lord, Jesus Christ". This was on my mind about these men who called out to their gods;

"Their jesus christ reminds me of our vordun. Both seem to be present when the sun warms your doorway and pleasant offerings are made in their honor. But as soon as you are taken prisoner and families ripped apart, they grow silent and disappear in the mist. When men and women cry out from their hell below the deck of a ship, the stench is so powerful no god will come near to hear their weeping."

Meanwhile, Billy Simms and the *Nelly* were riding the trade winds on a course outward bound for Liverpool. The ship, which had been so dangerously crowded with over three hundred men and women on board, now seemed huge and comfortable to her crew. Late at night, high above the deck working in the rigging, Billy felt the salt air at his back as he listened to the bow of the *Nelly* slicing easily through a calm sea. The low moon climbing out of the east relayed a soft glow from the water's surface. Simms was where he wanted to be and doing what he wanted to do. He loved the officers and crew of the *Nelly*. And, as he had now learned, he loved carrying his whip to sea when the Nelly would be moving sugar and slaves. God bless Captain Christopher and god bless the *Nelly*!

PRINCE of SAND - Chapter Six ... Vivre et mourir vite lent / Living Slow and Dying Fast

As I have said, the year of my birth was 1744. And now you understand that in 1760, when I was sixteen years old, the hand of fate twisted my life about in a most violent manner. Many years later I would learn of another man, also born in 1744, who was tempting the fates in a much different life than mine. This young man was a Jew, a Jew growing up in the German city of Frankfurt. As I struggled to survive in a world teaching me brutal new lessons, this German was developing plans to teach the world new lessons of his own. His name was Mayer Amschel Rothschild. The markets managed by European and African agents had caught me up in the midst of their trades. Call me Prince but, truth be told, I was but one unit of slave labor being traded in the island market of Saint Domingue. Markets, ships, slaves, brokers, products, counting houses, money changers – in 1760 I had no concept of such things but I was learning more than most, from the inside out, in the harshest school perfected by man over hundreds of years. Mayer Rothschild saw and understood these markets from a hilltop that I could not climb. His vision from that hilltop would sweep around the world. But it was early yet and we both still had much to learn.

"Lean into it lads! Put your bloody backs to it and *move* or each of your sorry arses will be mine before nine bells!"

It was now August of 1769 and the *Nelly* was in the island harbor of St. Croix loading eighty hogsheads of Virginia tobacco for shipment to Liverpool. Anderson the cook continued to serve as an effective task manager for certain activities. For eight years now, the *Nelly's* crew had managed her through six complete slaver voyages. Most of the crew had remained intact over the years, a tribute to Captain Christopher. As a matter of routine, the *Nelly* had continued to trade with Jaja in Annamaboe for the purchase of a full load of slaves. But the port favored for the sale of the slaves had been Recife in Brazil. Captain C always tried to keep the big decisions simple. Recife, as the eastern most major port in all of South America, presented the shortest voyage from Annamaboe so this made the Middle Passage as short as possible. As long as he could get a good price for his prisoners, the Captain reasoned that the less time spent with a full load of slaves below meant fewer slaves dead at sea, fewer crew members becoming ill and steadier profits as a result. Oddly, while many captains were intimidated by the cunning Jaja and chose to trade with him only out of necessity, Captain Christopher and Jaja had developed a reasonable business relationship. Captain C understood slaving's dangers. The greatest trading risk came in trying to purchase a full load of prisoners. Again, Captain C had focused on timing as his number one priority. Ships who spent months trying to gather slaves in small groups from multiple traders faced more chances for rebellion and longer periods carrying humans in filthy conditions. Slaving was brutal. If you failed to embrace this reality, the brutality of the trade would consume you. It was on their second voyage, in June of 1761, that Captain Christopher and Jaja had come to better understand one another. Nimba, Jaja's savage and trusted lieutenant, was with him as the two sat down in Jaja's meeting room to negotiate further with Captain Christopher and Helmsman Olson. Jaja was pushing rum around the table and praising the appearance of the *Nelly* when Captain C rather abruptly redirected the conversation;

"Jaja, as I am sure you remember, last year you delivered almost three hundred prisoners onto my ship in a single day. It was I, Jaja, I was the captain of that ship. Over many weeks at sea we carried the tribe that you had first loaded onto the *Cramoise*. My crew, Jaja, knows more about how Captain Roux and his men on the *Cramoise* met their end than any other group now at sea."

Both men were quiet as they stared at each other across the table. After a pause, Captain Christopher continued,

"I have been told that Captain Roux was often rude and insulting. It seems that he was unable to handle the tribe of prisoners you delivered to him in a manner that was ... safe."

Jaja's eyes narrowed somewhat before he slowly looked over to Nimba, seated to his right. Neither man displayed any emotion as Jaja returned his gaze to Christopher. Jaja spoke;

"Yes, we all learned that Captain Roux and his crew were not fully prepared for what Nimba and our men delivered. Fortunately, Nimba's men controlled the prisoners and your crew was successful in taking them to Saint Domingue. I congratulate you both."

Nimba nodded slightly, acknowledging the compliment, and stared at Captain C.

The captain spoke bluntly;

"Speed and safety. You, Jaja, have the force and systems in place to deliver hundreds of slaves quickly. The *Nelly* and her crew have demonstrated the ability to safely board a large group and to clear the harbor in the same day. We both choose to play this dangerous game. The *Nelly* will need a full load of slaves every year or so when we enter the Annamaboe harbor. We want to spend as little time as possible with you and Nimba and to sail westward as quickly as we can. The *Nelly* will pay a good price for such treatment. And Jaja, we keep our mouths shut about how we trade for our slaves. My men will fight to the death for each other but they care little to nothing about anyone else."

Jaja remained silent and passive before smiling slightly;

"Yes, Captain, we both understand this business. For us, the prettiest sight of you and your ship is when you are leaving our shores. Best for us is when you leave with a full load taken from our cages after we have unloaded your goods and drink your rum. Our men are most happy when you leave."

Nimba added;

"And my men have shown they too will fight and kill for each other. Traders who understand this will have more success than did the captain of the French ship."

Captain Christopher responded right away;

"Yes, we both have good and loyal men ready to deal with danger. Our goal is always to leave quickly. Jaja, get us full loads and we will be gone on the tide. And Nimba, our good men will have no need to spill each other's blood."

Jaja and Nimba exchanged a quick glance and nodded in agreement. Four men drank their rum.

After a successful Middle Passage from Annamaboe to Recife in the summer of 1769, the *Nelly* was committed to stop in the port of St. Croix in the Virgin Islands on her homeward bound leg to Liverpool. Only five hundred miles from Saint Domingue, Captain Christopher could have easily included a stop in Port Au Prince but he had no desire to return to the place where one of his men had been murdered. The *Nelly* would load the Virginia tobacco her owners had contracted for and then set sail for Liverpool. Veteran seamen were wary of being in this part of the world during August and September when the enormous storms called hurricanes were known to rise up on the eastern horizon.

"Excuse me, lad, but might you announce me to the manager of this office? My name is Captain Andrew Christopher, in command of the *Nelly* out of Liverpool." Captain Christopher had moments earlier come down the gangway from the *Nelly* onto the docks of St. Croix as his men secured lines and began to prepare the ship to take on cargo. He had been directed to the office of Beekman and Cruger Ltd. that was conveniently located in the midst of St. Croix's trading center. Beekman and Cruger Ltd. was a counting house owned primarily by the Cruger family from the North American colony of New York. It was Beekman and Cruger that served as the agent for arranging this shipment of Virginia tobacco that the *Nelly* would carry to Liverpool. Captain Christopher was hoping to find the principal of the St. Croix office, Mr.

Nicholas Cruger.

Captain C looked about the well appointed office. Actually, he was a bit surprised to find a youngster seated at what seemed to be the primary trading desk. Perhaps he was the son of one of the clerks and was enjoying a few moments in his father's chair while he was away.

The youngster rose and began to speak, "Good morning Captain Christopher, and welcome to St. Croix. My name is Alexander Hamilton and, as assistant manager of Beekman and Cruger in St. Croix, let me congratulate you on your safe arrival. We have, of course, anticipated the arrival of the *Nelly* and have scheduled an orderly loading of the eighty hogsheads of Virginia tobacco to commence tomorrow morning at eight bells, assuming sir, that such an arrangement meets with your approval."

Captain C tried to hide his surprise as he focused on the boy in front of him, "Master Hamilton, forgive me as I was advised to ask for Mr. Cruger. Thank you for your kind welcome and yes, commencing the loading at eight bells will be most satisfactory as we hope to be loaded and outward bound for Liverpool within three days time." He studied this confident and well spoken youngster who had now stepped out from the desk to extend his hand to the Captain;

"Of course, Captain, I understand that you would be expecting Mr. Cruger to meet you here this morning. Mr. Cruger is currently in Charleston as his presence was required there at the request of the Harbor Master following an unfortunate incident with a sizable three ship cargo of mules bound for Cuban sugarcane plantations. In his absence, I can assure that we have put all matters in order to assure the satisfactory transfer of this cargo of tobacco to the *Nelly* as per your contract executed in Liverpool. It is now a routine responsibility of mine to serve as manager of our office when Mr. Cruger is required to travel. Your bills of lading have been prepared and are ready for review at your convenience, sir."

Captain C responded, "I understand and thank you for your diligence on our behalf, Master Hamilton. Is your Mr. Cruger required to travel out of St. Croix often?"

"Well, sir, his father and other family members operate the business from New York while Mr. Cruger was spending the majority of his time here in St. Croix. Our growth, however, has been such that he is increasingly called on to represent our interests in certain ports of call and I, your honor, am a beneficiary of his travels as I manage our office in his absence."

"I see. And is he often in Charleston?"

Young Hamilton nodded, "Aye, Charleston is quite active for Beekman and Cruger as we enjoy a particularly agreeable relationship with our trading partner there, the office of Begbie and Barnwell. Mr. Cruger would most certainly be here to personally welcome you, Captain, had not such a large number of the mules presented to our Charleston agent for shipment been found to be, well ... on the brink of eternity, shall we say. Perhaps he may return before your departure which I am certain would please him greatly."

"Yes, well, no need for further explanation. We all understand the uncertainties of our trade. My Helmsman, Mr. Olson, will be handling all preparations with your staff which I am certain will be acceptable in every detail. My thanks to you, again, Master Hamilton."

"At your service, Captain."

Captain C left the office with the slightest shake of his head. Yes, I am growing older in this work, he thought, but good God, boys managing the trade offices and directing the exchange of cargo? Well, he had to admit, his own Billy Simms could hardly see over the bulkhead on the *Abundance* when he had leapt overboard and paddled out to help rescue seaman Tom Jackson back in '54. I guess some just take to it sooner than others, he mumbled, as he headed for the warehouse to look over the tobacco.

The crew would be busy over the coming days with both the supplies needed to prepare the *Nelly* for her return voyage to Liverpool as well as the tobacco to be loaded for this last leg home. Billy Simms was, as usual, happy in his work as he now ranked as one of the senior crew aboard the *Nelly*. Simms was still a young man but he had now been fourteen years – over half his life – at sea with Captain C. No one knew the *Nelly* as well as Simms and he always welcomed a visit to a new port. This trip was Billy's fifth or sixth Middle Passage. He had to sit down and count them out to be certain. The miseries of the lower deck never changed while his pleasure in having young slave girls of his choice to service his quarters had become a ritual. Simms tried not to let his mind wander to such places when he was busy. No, when he wrapped the strands of his whip around the handle and put it away, he tried to put those memories away in the same drawer. Besides, he always knew that he would again be reaching for both, the whip and the memories, soon enough.

Billy found himself thinking of Liverpool. They should be home by October, certainly November. The boy, Peter, would be eight this year. He had been born while Billy was on the *Nelly's* maiden voyage. Simms would have named him Christopher, after the good Captain, but Janet was there on her own and she had called him Peter. Billy figured he would call the next one Christopher. It had been almost two years later, in 1762, when Janet had a second child but Christopher was no name for a girl. The daughter was named Nancy. Billy tried to imagine how things would be with Janet and the two children once he reached Liverpool. He was certain that the three of them would be on the dock when he arrived and it was a given that their two rooms would be scrubbed as clean as the deck of the *Nelly*. Beyond that, he had no idea what to expect. Nancy and Peter Simms were born and raised by their mother. They would know little of their father and he less about them. What they did learn about Billy Simms scared the hell out of them.

The months spent for repair and refitting of the ship in Liverpool between voyages defined the changes in Billy's life and the lives of his family. Returning from sea after the better part of a year's absence, he would reclaim a role as head of a family accustomed to life as three souls caring for each other as best they could. When the fourth member arrived on the docks, the rhythm of the Simms family would always change and seldom for the better. The caring for one another, this would always haunt Billy Simms. The children, Peter and Nancy, now eight and six in 1769, naturally loved their mother who cared for them as best she could. Janet raised them in the same poverty she had always known and the youngsters did not know the difference. Instinctively, they felt they should care for their father just as they loved their mother, but in this their family puzzle was always missing a piece. Plain and simple, Billy Simms did not care for anyone unless they sailed with him on the *Nelly*. Did he know or understand this truth? Who can say? But his children feared more than loved him and Janet was unable to bridge the awkward gaps. Holding them each by the hand as the crew of the *Nelly* was taking leave from the ship, she urged them,

"Peter, Nancy, your father be comin' onto the docks now. Look up and be happy to be a-seein' him. Smile real sweet now."

Billy walked toward them with his canvas bag of belongings slung lightly over his shoulder. His face was calm and without expression. He stopped as Janet stepped to him. She put her arms around him, kissed him on the cheek and then stepped back;

"Well, a good day to ya seaman Billy Simms and welcome home! You have two fine young-uns awful happy today and a fine leg o' mutton a-waitin' for ya' on your table."

The father managed a slight grin and nodded his head as he stared down at Peter and Nancy Simms. Other families reunited after such a long separation were locked in embraces, holding on to each other as they laughed, all speaking over each other at once. For the Simms, outside of Janet's natural ability to break the ice, there was nary a word uttered. Peter was old enough to recognize his father and he warily eyed him, hoping for some gesture of pleasure and recognition. Billy simply looked the boy up and down, nodded some more and handed off his bag for Peter to carry. Peter would not remember if his father had touched him, although Billy may have put a hand on his shoulder. The little girl, Nancy, had almost no recollection of this man as she remained close to her mother with one hand gripping Janet's skirt. Billy seemed to freeze when he saw her, as if he had only then realized that she was his daughter. He then bent down and, as he reached out his hand, spoke quietly,

"My, you are a pretty little one."

Nancy pulled back, unsure about this man now reaching for her. Janet, hoping that the girl would go to her father, gently pulled her arm toward Billy,

"Now go on, Nancy, and hug your father who has been so long on ship to come see ya."

But both Billy and Nancy had stepped back.

"No, no – it's all right", Billy mumbled. "She'll be needin' time to come to know her father."

You could see the relief on the faces of both father and daughter. With this most awkward reunion behind them, the four of them turned and began their short walk home. Nancy would later speak of that moment as the first clear memory she had of her father, an oddly quiet man who was quick to anger. He often commented that he saw her as attractive yet he made no public show of affection toward daughter or son. They arrived at their two rooms soon enough. The tiny space was so clean Janet could have served the mutton on her scrubbed floors. The children were put in the bed they shared early that evening. Billy placed his few pieces of clothing in a wooden box on the floor in the corner. Janet watched as he slipped his whip under their bed, easily within his reach.

Yes, it was 1769 and life enslaved on a plantation in Saint-Domingue was painfully slow. Nothing ever changed. I had arrived in Port Au Prince a sixteen year-old boy. The market price was paid for me in 1761. Eight years of me had been delivered. Looking at me you saw a man, an old man, who knew much about slavery and nothing of freedom. Yes, it is true that I could still remember growing up free in a family and tribe that generally supported one another in all things. But make no mistake – as an adult, I had not spent a single day, not a single hour as a free man. Truth be known, I could not tell you how it felt to be a free man. The days were as one. Long, dirty, wet with sweat and damp from the rains – and hungry. You went to work with the sun and the sun was forever in the sky. The heat was heavy on you. The food, brought in buckets into the fields, was grotesque. Slowly you moved through the field.

Long powerful strokes with the curved machete angled correctly into the sugarcane stalk at the proper height would cleanly fell a stalk with a single blow. Slowly you moved the cane onto the piles where the carts would be loaded. Slashing often with little attention to technique and hurrying from one pile to another marked an ignorant man and ignorance cost thousands their lives in the sugarcane. Slowly you cut the cane and slowly

you tried to get through the day. Food in such heat did not seem to matter much until you returned to the huts at sunset. Gathering yourself at day's end and trying to recover from the fields, your constant companion was the hunger. Great effort would be made to try and trade for something extra, something decent. Bananas, a chicken or a piece of fresh fish, something unspoiled that was most satisfying. But there was never enough. Constant hunger more than weakens the body, it ruins the mind. There is nowhere to hide from the hunger. Deep within, you know there is nothing to be done. Being hungry today is hard. But knowing that you will still be hungry tomorrow is what crushes you. Once you are broken, only part of the suffering has to do with the lack of food.

One similarity did remind me of my African home – no white men were among us. As a boy, I had never seen the ocean or the white man. Black men captured, traded and brought me out to the coast where I was sold to white men and rode the waves for months in one of their three mast ships. After being sold in Port Au Prince and delivered to the fields, black men told me when to wake and sleep. I worked with black men and women, often cried and seldom laughed with them, was beaten and whipped by black overseers and nursed to health by them when sick. All so I could work some more in the fields. White men may have owned us but none came to see us. Over those eight years, slaves went into the fields and sugarcane came out. How the sugarcane was processed and the sugar sold, such was the owners' concern. How the cane was actually gathered from the fields was left to the black slaves who died trying. Eight years of me had been delivered and consumed. Most men at age twenty-four are young and beginning their lives. My youth had dissolved on the beaches of Annamaboe, just as a lump of sugar dissolves in a cup of hot tea. Rarely was I near a mirror or pane of glass, but reflections reach us regardless. It was not easy to look at myself and deal with what the cane fields had taken from me over those years. Living in frustration and loss over such a long time, I wanted something for myself that I still controlled.

My plan to leave was a long time coming. As a slave, I first racked my brain over plans that would deliver me into freedom. But that was the problem – there was no place to go that offered any true hope for freedom. If you run from the plantation, where do you go? Trying to hide from everyone on Saint-Domingue would just be another prison under a different name. To leave the island, you needed to be on a boat. The likelihood that a runaway would gain passage on a ship was so remote that you never really thought about the next step. Where would you go on your escape?

Name a port where a fugitive from slavery arrives as a free man. In Saint-Domingue, the domination of slaves was so complete the slaveholders had laws to try and take even our gods away from us. Something called the Code Noir was in place to try and keep us from practicing our own religions. All slaveholders were expected to convert us to the religion they called Catholic within eight days of our arrival. In this strange and horrible place, such an absurd idea actually struck me as being funny. The same man who had purchased my body was now going to "convert" my mind over my first eight days in his hell? Really, you wonder what all their fuss was about and it made me laugh bitterly. Slaves just secretly pooled their religions and became unified in maintaining our own gods. Worship of Vordun became known as Vodou. It was amusing to watch. Images of what the Catholic called saints were used to represent various Vodou spirits to convince these worshippers of Catholic that we worshipped the Catholic too. How stupid. And to what purpose? Day in and day out, you were pushed in and out of the fields until months became years and you were dead. I just shook my head and had to laugh. Can anyone tell me why some owner would give a shit about what some slave cutting the cane was thinking about before he died? None of this talk of gods meant a thing to me. For me, all who bothered about it, slave and owner alike, were wasting their time.

Eight years in the sugarcane - I was old and growing older. Your mind had nowhere to go. It was time to leave. My memory of family had given way to images of what I thought they might have been and it had all begun to dissolve and fade away. Sometimes, in the dark hours when you can hardly recall the afternoon but are unable to see tomorrow, I was closer to my mother than I had ever been before yet I was not certain it was she. You think of something that seems important before you think some more. Nothing is important. Something that is a long time coming never arrives. The pitiful men and women joining me in the fields, they were empty. None of them had anything. I saw nothing I desired except in those who had left and I envied their leaving. I was jealous that they could leave. But they all had to make a trade to leave and the only trader doing business was death.

Ready to make my trade, I studied on the best method. Cutting myself open to bleed to death or getting to the shore to be drowned in the sea, they both worried me. It seemed that the pain would be great and there would be a chance that some fool would get in the way and try to 'save' me. To make the effort and suffer the pain only to end up still alive would be cruel and unacceptable. Time and again, I came to the conclusion that death by hanging would be best. When a man is hung, he rarely chokes to death. The best method is to fall far and hard enough to break the neck and deliver death in a relatively fast and painless manner. The correct amount of strong rope, a large limb high enough to provide a long fall to snap the neck and an out of the way location – this was an arrangement that I could control. Once this decision was made, my miserable life actually seemed to improve. Knowing you have a plan that can be successful and keeping secret possession of that plan is uplifting. Somehow I felt smarter - smarter than I had been before and smarter than those around me who could not figure out how to leave. Smarter than the owner who had no idea that I was getting ready to leave. Just walking about with such a secret was important to me and made me feel different. For those who have next to nothing, a secret plan   even a plan to die   can become what they value most.

The Royer family plantation was enormous spreading over more than 1,600 acres. I had been told that the family home and their surrounding buildings were quite grand. The disgusting huts that I knew were miles from the family quarters, which I never saw, and were somewhat less than grand. The plantation operated around the large river, the Artibonite River, which flowed through the property. The river brought value to the land and the plantation managers developed a network of irrigation canals and reservoir ponds to extend and control the reach of the river over this vast acreage. When I was not cutting cane, I was digging irrigation ditches. Both were back breaking tasks as we were pushed without mercy by other slaves, the overseers, whose only mission in life was to drive enough production from us in order to keep themselves in their favored jobs. I have told you of the horrors of being held below deck on a slave ship. While I was now outdoors most of the time and understood where I would be each day, the misery of the unspeakable conditions and the pure pain endured to complete the endless work sucked life out of men and women faster than you could count the dead. Watching the dead leave, no longer forced to kneel under the lash or crawl out of a hut before dawn and be marched into the fields, my decision to join them made great sense to me.

While I never saw the family estate, the plantation was so large there were three different mills and boiling houses to handle all of the cane and I was often sent to help unload the carts at one of the mills. The mill machinery was housed within a two-story windmill with a large covered storage area attached. The cut sugarcane was unloaded and stacked in the storage area. The mill machinery, powered by the windmill, crushed the cane stalks forcing out the juice that was collected and sent over to the boiling house. Making sugar requires some skill. In the boiling house, the slave who tests the sticky syrup between his fingers or by dipping his elbow is know as the boiler. Experienced boilers were counted on to know exactly when the sugar was ready to set. Stokers had the dangerous and miserable job of keeping the fires burning all day, every day over the production season that ran for almost six months of the year. We were always hearing stories about those who suffered terrible burns or died in boiler house accidents. Like I said, I often moved cane around the mill but I made sure to stay away from the boiler house. The fields were as close to hell as I planned to travel.

The mill was another place where plenty of slaves were injured but at least they did not have to work around the roaring fires of the boiler house all day and night. The windmill turned the machinery that crushed the cane and the process ran constantly. Such work becomes routine and that was when the danger was great. As long as the stalks are being fed into the press, all is well. When something that is not supposed to be mixed in with the stalks reaches the press, problems erupt. The mill foreman would raise hell if a machete or rake went into the press and fouled the machinery but there were times when the item caught in the press was human. Rest your hand too long on the next stack of sugarcane ready to be crushed or allow a loose piece of your ragged clothing to be snagged in the stalks and you would watch in horror as the press drew your hand or arm into the unforgiving press. Stopping the press – that was the problem. Think about trying to stop a windmill. It is not going to happen. Feeling yourself being pulled forward and knowing part of your body was now going to be crushed, such was the danger always lurking in the mill.

It was getting late in the season, October of 1769, when one of the men I often worked with had his arm trapped in the press. I was sent to the mill less than an hour after the accident. He was still there, stretched out in an empty cart, while they worked to stop the bleeding. His left arm, from the elbow down, no longer resembled an arm or hand. The mangled flesh hung from the elbow like a rag. The man was unconscious, a good thing, and he was moved to the boiler house where they amputated at the elbow. There were plenty of red hot irons to choose from and tar available for sealing the wound. About three months later, early in the new year, it occurred to me that this cripple would not be sent back into the fields. The man had lost half of his left arm and he was leaving the fields. Leaving the fields. Right then, right there my plans had changed. I still had secret possession of a plan and I was confident that I could control the plan. But now the trade I had on my mind was different. No prayers would be offered to Vordun. It never crossed my mind to wonder what the woman Sanja, my mother, would think of my plan. It seemed that I had been alone and on my own for more than a lifetime. My plan presented many problems that I could not yet answer but what did I have to lose? There was much planning and preparation for me to begin. And there was something to live for.

PRINCE of SAND - Chapter Seven ... C'est le Moment de Partir / Time to Move

Study a map of western Europe. Select one city that is centrally located and many people would point to Frankfurt. Almost equal distance from London, Paris and Vienna, if your business objective was to create centers of influence and you planned to direct your efforts from a hub where you could be most effective, Frankfurt would be a logical choice. The Jews of Frankfurt made up one particular group who, by 1750, had found Frankfurt to be a city where they might prosper, in spite of the restrictions that the city enforced. The Jewish ghetto, known as the Judengasse, was surrounded by walls and separated from the rest of the city.

Many years earlier the city had limited entry by Jews to five hundred families and a new arrival had to posses at least 1,000 guilders. The Judengasse was a crowded narrow alley – a village within a city. Three gates, the north and south gates and a middle gate on the western side known as the Judenbruckchen, were locked every night and on Sundays and religious holidays. The city of Frankfurt would open her gates to the Jews only for workdays and even then approved occupations for them were limited. Over hundreds of years, the European Jewish community had developed expertise and a level of acceptance as moneychangers and bankers. Such was the case in Frankfurt where a few small banking houses were Jewish owned and operated.

It was a fine summer morning, the weather clear and cooler than normal. The year was 1770. The beautiful day provided the perfect setting for the wedding that was to take place within the Judengasse. The ceremony was much anticipated within this close-knit community as the city, consistent with their restrictive policies regarding the Jews, only permitted twelve Jewish weddings each year. The groom, a native of Frankfurt, had moved from the city years earlier to Hanover in order to apprentice in currency exchange and foreign trade with the respected banking firm of Simon Wolf Oppenheimer. The young man, now twenty-six, had recently returned. The bride had only celebrated her sixteenth birthday four months earlier. Her father, Wolf Salomon Schnapper, had a small bank in Frankfurt and Gutle Schnapper would draw on her family's banking expertise quite often over the coming years as she consulted with her husband on many business related matters. Before this day was out, Gutle Schnapper would become Mrs. Mayer Amschel Rothschild. In 1770, no one could know that she would bear him nineteen children, ten of who would survive into adulthood. Gutle Rothschild would live to be almost one hundred years old. In her lifetime she would help her five sons as they spread out over Europe to execute their parents' plan in establishing a banking empire whose wealth and influence would exceed all of their expectations. From relatively humble beginnings in the Judengasse, Gutle and Mayer Amschel Rothschild began their journey together in 1770. Before the end of her life, Gutle Rothschild would be known as the matriarch of one of the wealthiest families in the world.

Mayer Amschel Rothschild and I may have both been born in 1744 but we were taking significantly different paths in August of 1770. If you were privy to their wedding day musings, you might have heard Mayer Amschel whisper,

"Gutle, so young and beautiful, draw on my strength as I take rest in your arms. We have much to be grateful for and so much more that we can see before us. Family, Gutle, family will surround us – our family – and refuge will forever be the deep well to be drawn on by us and ours. Our family will draw from our strength and they will forever find refuge within the house of Rothschild."

My plan, for now, included no one but myself but I can tell you it was no less ambitious than that of the couple in Frankfurt. The Rothschilds, feet firmly planted in Austria, were poised to take bold steps forward across Europe. Yamar, long separated from my village on the Dahomey plain and long known as Prince, had no footing. My feet were mired in the muddy hole that was the sugar plantation. There would be no bold steps forward unless and until I invented some means by which to crawl out from that hole, the grave that was closing in around me. You crawl before you walk. You crawl on your hands and on your knees.

Early in the year I had begun to complete various chores in a different manner. No one paid any attention to my method. I have always favored my right hand and naturally used it more regularly than my left. Increasingly, I used my stronger hand and arm almost exclusively. For obvious two-handed tasks, my left hand was relied upon only as a guide to provide but minimal support. Later, I actually began to bind fingers on my left hand together forcing them to function as one. My goal was to teach my brain to understand how to operate with a limited left hand. You might refer to someone as a cripple and then be amazed at his or her expertise in completing difficult tasks. Who is crippled? Who can accomplish difficult tasks? It was also my goal to use my ability to speak the French as much as I could. Slaves who survive learn to keep their eyes down and their mouths shut. Out of necessity, it was my practice to keep quiet. Now I looked for opportunities to speak the French often. While I was careful to stay out of any trouble I used the French as often as I could. If I could maneuver out of the fields, I would need to show that I could prove my value elsewhere. Speaking the French, perhaps I could talk my way to help my owner by getting on a ship and find my "elsewhere" far from this island. My ability to see a way out was blurred, my plan lacked definition but first things first – I would leave the sugarcane. I had no choice. Leave the fields of 'cane or die trying.

For years I had been surviving as an individual. By now I understood it, had come to accept it and I was determined, if at all possible, to operate from a position of strength. Such an objective, after being resigned to seek death by ones own hand, may seem inconsistent but that is not so. The gambler quietly looks for an advantage, prepared to move boldly if the reward might outweigh the risk. Prepared to move boldly to leave the plantation, my original plan had now evolved. True, there was little to no strength from which to draw upon as I took my position, other than strength from within. Did I have such strength, strength enough to crawl out from this hole? Who knew? But I was not afraid to find out. Not knowing was a luxury I decided I could not afford. Lots had been cast and I was weary of playing a losing game. My mind was beyond the pain and I needed to know if I would win or lose. I was desperate to learn the answer.

The summer was drawing to a close. My health was as good as I could expect. I felt strong but, looking back, I believe it was because I had a plan. Some hope had crept into my mind. Four of us had loaded two large carts that were now overloaded with 'cane. Two mules slowly pulled the carts drawing all of us closer to the mill. The sun was low on the horizon as we crested the small rise that brought us up onto the long field with the windmill clearly visible at the far end. Slowly turning, the blades of the mill seemed to reel us in across the field. Months of practice had brought me here with a strong right arm and a left hand much ignored. My French was better, at least more familiar, as I had been speaking often. The carts were brought to a halt in the area where the sugarcane was unloaded. There were a few familiar faces of those who regularly worked at the mill and some lazy waves of acknowledgement were exchanged. Everything seemed to be moving so slowly. It was something of a surprise to me that I felt rather calm. The routine of unloading the 'cane and the monotony of watching the stalks being fed into the press left little room for drama. After sharing in the task of unloading the carts, I wandered into the enclosed area where the 'cane was squeezed into the press. The foreman, a light colored slave who had taken the white name Ricardo, stood near the machinery with an air of importance about him as he watched the stalks being pushed toward the press. After a few minutes had passed, something caught Ricardo's attention. Turning his back to the press, he walked about twenty feet away from his spot. Now was the time and I moved without hesitation. The sun had just set and the light inside was not as bright as it had been just a few minutes earlier. Casually I shuffled ahead toward the press with the supply of stalks being fed forward positioned on my left. I walked within six feet of the press after angling to my left until I was an arm's length from the stalks. The constant sound of the stalks reaching the press and methodically being crushed seemed to block out any other noise. I had picked out a clump of stalks that were about to be drawn into the machine and simply stared at the spot where I would place my hand. This was the moment. Lightly kicking my right foot into my left, I pretended to trip slightly and bent forward shooting my left hand out and onto the sugarcane pretending to regain my balance. I was very careful not to actually put my weight on my left hand. I would not lose control and watch my entire arm be drawn into the relentless press. My plan was always to try and have the two fingers on the left side of that hand crushed into the press just as I moved back sufficiently to my right in order to assure that nothing more of me would be destroyed. For one brief moment, before my senses took over, I remember wondering why I felt no pain.

It was the middle of the night when I regained consciousness. Soon I could recall some of what had happened. As the sound of my left hand being crushed had reached my ears, a wave of pain shot up my arm just as an enormous clap of thunder follows a bolt of lightening. My eyes must have rolled up into my head. Luck was with me as I had dropped to my knees and then fell onto my right side, away from the press. The injury to the left side of my hand would never be reversed but the damage had been limited to three fingers. Over half of the middle finger was cut away. The two smaller fingers were completely gone as was part of the palm that had supported the little finger. Fortunately, the forefinger and thumb remained and would continue to serve me well over the years ahead. As I expected, I had been moved to the nearby boiler house where the mangled flesh was cut away. The remainder of my left hand had been roughly stitched together and bandaged with a piece of cloth. The pain was overwhelming. The throbbing sensation was constant and I was weak from the loss of blood. Someone decided that I would remain at the boiler house for the next few days sleeping in one of the bunks that were kept for workers who stayed there working long shifts in the production season. It made no difference where I stayed – I had no possessions and my hut was miserable. Food was somewhat better at the boiler house and I was allowed to sleep for a couple of days. Permission to rest was strange after eight years in the 'cane.

After being sent back to the huts, I was ordered to work at the shed where the machetes and other tools were locked up each night. Food buckets and water bags were also stored there after slaves returned from the fields each evening. I was to work on repairing tools, cleaning out the buckets and rising early to fill the water bags each morning. The work was boring but much easier than the miserable life in the fields. I had two very real concerns that were now constantly on my mind. The first was trying to keep my wound as clean as possible and free from rot. Open wounds and rotting flesh were common in the sugarcane fields. Trying to keep a wound clean in the fields was impossible. Working at the shed, at least I was able to take a few minutes each day to remove the cloth from my hand and let it dry in the sun. I believe this saved me from the rot. The second matter that kept me awake at night was concern that I would be sent back into the fields. While I worked with my injured hand to try and regain strength, it was important to be recognized as a cripple unfit for cutting the 'cane. Cruel beyond measure would be my fate if I were to suffer such an injury only to be marched back into the fields. My next move would need to come soon. It was time to move.

Over the eight years on the plantation I had only become close to a few others. People around you died often. New arrivals were scared or angry. Anyone who appeared to be a troublemaker was beaten harshly and often. There was nothing to be shared amongst us other than misery and I had all of that I could stomach. The windmill and the boiler house had been built close to one of the canals that led into the Artibonite River. This made it possible for the owner to move his sugar directly from the boiler house to his warehouses in Port Au Prince. During my time in the fields, I had not only dug the irrigation ditches but I learned much about the system used to flood the fields and regulate the flow into the canals. Now I regularly volunteered to help cart the cut stalks to the windmill and help move the sacks of sugar down to the canal. It became my mission to convince the overseer that I could be valuable in helping on the barges that carried the sugar to Port Au Prince. Tasks away from the fields and near the water, this was my focus. Fortunately, the level of the canal was often low and men were needed from time to time to help manage the irrigation ditches in order to increase the flow into the canal. Understanding the system and ready to climb into the muddy ditches to help get the water redirected, I was ordered to work on a barge carrying a full load of sugar to Port Au Prince. One very important move was about to take place! I was going to be in Port Au Prince and there were always large ships in Port Au Prince.

As I made moves to try and change my pitiful situation, others hoped to keep things going just the way they were. In Liverpool, Billy Simms was not so much taking steps with a growing family as he was being pulled along the way. For a few years, his wife Janet made an effort to bring her family of four together as one unit but Billy never really understood how to fit in. It was probably a better question to ask why he kept coming back year after year but he was clearly a creature of habit and he preferred a set routine, just as long as that routine always led him back for a long stretch at sea. Janet predictably grew weary of the effort and, in time, left Billy Simms to himself. It seemed everyone was happier that way and the two children were always sure to give their father a wide berth. Peter was a quiet and rather awkward boy. This was just the opposite from his younger sister, Nancy, who was both bright and outgoing from an early age. From time to time, out of necessity, Janet would bring the little girl to the tavern while she worked. As soon as she came out from the kitchen or caught the eye of a customer, it was only a matter of time before she would have customers asking her to sing them a song or tell them a story about her doll. Nancy brightened any room. She was a pretty girl and was always direct and respectful in her manner. Like her mother, Nancy Simms laughed easily and never seemed to cry or complain as young children so often do. This little girl carried herself well beyond her years and adults welcomed her company. Billy Simms barely noticed his children. He seemed to be vaguely aware of their presence while his focus was forever placed on his preparations to help take the *Nelly* back to sea. By the time Nancy had reached ten years of age, she could recall having watched her father ship out on five different slaver voyages. The girl worried that she might be punished if someone discovered her true feelings – that she now looked forward to Billy Simms' departures and always dreaded his return.

Barges from the various plantations moved down the Artibonite River loaded with large sacks of sugar ready to be stored in the long low warehouses lined up near the docks. Slaves who could help keep the barges moving and protect the valuable cargo remained on this important job. There were only a few of us selected so I tried to learn everything I could about getting the sugar from the mill and boiler house safely to the Port Au Prince warehouses. All those sacks of sugar would be shipped out of Saint Domingue. Somehow I would find a way to join them. After three trips down river to Port Au Prince and back I had learned a lot about how the sugar ended up in the holds of the large ships bound for distant ports. It was the spring of 1771 and, at age twenty-six, I had begun to feel more like the young man that I was as my body and my mind tried to recuperate from the hell of working in the 'cane every day. Having tasted my escape from the fields, now the fear that I would be sent back began to haunt me terribly. Going back would mean death. All of my senses were drawn to getting back to Port Au Prince and finding some way onto a ship. The next barge loaded and launched for Port Au Prince was my fourth trip to the docks. My French was improving steadily as my new circumstances exposed me to many more conversations. I was helping move sugar sacks from the wharf into the warehouse when I overheard the conversation that changed my life. The manager of the Royer family warehouses, Mr. Pascal, was gesturing to a seaman that he obviously knew well,

"Nicolas, dites-moi." … "Nicolas, please tell me. How in the hell am I supposed to manage our arrangements for the shipment of hundreds of tons of sugar to all points east, keep enough warehouse space available for the enormous amount of sugar arriving on the barges and still take time to meet the ship arriving next week in St. Croix delivering six slaves from Cuba that Mr. Royer traded for last month? I am but one man! They seem to think I can just jump on our schooner that runs to St. Croix, take possession of the slaves and come directly back home without any interruption to our operation. This is madness! No, I simply cannot be gone from these docks. Not now, anyway."

Nicolas Dumas, a native creole Port Au Prince sailor and sometime merchant who often handled matters of trade for the Royer family, replied to his friend, Samuel Pascal,

"Alright now Samuel, calm yourself. We will figure something out – we always do. I agree that this is not a good time for you to be away from Port Au Prince. The amount of sugar shipping out from these docks is more than anyone ever thought possible. Let me speak with Mr. Royer and suggest that I make the run to St. Croix in your place. Would that work for you, my friend?"

"Yes, yes of course that would work. But the other part of my problem is their requirement that one of my men accompany me to help make sure we always have control of the new slaves. Sending another man makes good sense. It is just that the timing is terrible. My crew is already stretched to the limit. My hands are tied", was Sam Pascal's response.

Dumas smiled as he put a hand on Pascal's shoulder, "Well I have to believe that Mr. Royer, with all his many men and resources, can find a man to help me keep six niggers in line on the short run back from St. Croix. I'll plan to speak with him tomorrow."

Pascal already looked relieved and allowed himself a slight smile. The two friends seemed to be in a good mood so I quickly decided to take a chance, hoping that what I was about to say would not be taken as an unwelcome intrusion and land me in serious trouble. I stood within ten feet of Mr. Pascal and, bowing from the waste, made the following statement,

"Excusez-moi, monsieur Pascal"... "Excuse me, Mr. Pascal. My apology for speaking to you directly, sir, but I am a new man moving sugar on the windmill barge and I could not help but hear that you may have need for another of Monsieur Royer's slaves. Of course, your honor, it is not for me to say where I should work but as the new man on the barge, I am still learning the job." I quickly glanced at Nicolas Dumas as I suggested, "Perhaps my overseer would not care if I was to be sent on a ship to help return cargo from St. Croix?"

Just like that, the words were out of my mouth and the two men had turned their heads and stared at me. The sun was very hot and no breeze was stirring. I could feel the sweat rolling down across my temples and the sting as some of it found a way into the far corners of my eyes. By squinting and blinking hard, I tried to move the sweat further down onto my cheeks. But I recall feeling good about speaking up. If they did their worse, what would happen? I would be slapped around and told to shut the hell up. Slaves in my world handled such beatings regularly and with nothing at all to gain. At least in this chance meeting I had some possibility of maybe finding a way to get onto a ship.

It seemed to take a long time before Dumas raised one of his eyes toward me and asked, "Where did you learn your French, boy? And tell me, have you worked at all in handling other slaves?"

His manner was easy. Not so hard as many who brutally worked the slaves like me. My mind was racing but the word "calm" kept rolling through my head. I tried to appear calm as I shared a piece of my story,

"When I was a boy on the Dahomey plain in Africa my father and a few other leaders of our tribe regularly spoke the French with traders. He taught me and as I grew older we often spoke only the French to try and learn more. As to handling other slaves, eight years I have survived cutting the Royer sugarcane. Yes, your honor, I have experience with other slaves."

Dumas turned to Pascal and shrugged his shoulders as he turned up his palms. But Pascal eyed me hard and, glancing at my left hand, asked sharply,

"What the hell happened to your hand?"

Calm was on my mind and quietly I said, "Loading 'cane into the press at the windmill, I was shoved forward when another man stumbled. But the hand healed well and I am strong." And now I lied again, "I spent some time working on the ships at Annamaboe before being sent here to Saint-Domingue."

Dumas asked, "What do they call you?"

"Prince", I replied.

"Prince? … Well, to me you're 'Dr. P'. So here you are, Samuel. Get the fucking barge master over there to swap out Dr. P here and I will take him with me over to St. Croix. He speaks the language, which can be helpful, and the two of us can certainly handle five or six slaves already in chains." Looking at me, he added, "And you *will* do everything I tell you to do. Am I right, Dr. P?"

"Absolutely, your honor. Absolutely", was all I could think to say.

Eight years in the fields had seemed like eighty. Now things were moving quickly. Dumas had business at the plantation the next day. Apparently nobody seemed to care one-way or another who joined him on the short trip to St. Croix. I was still moving sugar sacks in Port Au Prince when Nicolas returned two days later. He came toward me as if I was just one more nigger on the docks, which I was, and casually mentioned,

"Well Dr. P, gather your things together in a small bag that you can hang on the end of a hammock. Be ready tomorrow at 6:00 a.m. We sail with the tide."

He was already well past me as I mumbled, "Not to worry about a bag, your honor. I don't own anything. And thank you, sir. Thank you mightily."

If I slept at all that night I remembered nothing of it. The two masts of the Royer schooner would load sail the next morning and I would be on that ship, with permission, outward bound for St. Croix! Boarding a ship that some white captain and crew would be sailing had been the worse nightmare of my shitty life. So strange, now it would be happening again and I knew it represented my only hope to survive. Still, the thought of climbing back onto a ship filled me with fear. Images of the hundreds who had been crammed with me below decks on the *Nelly* never left me. The smell was there forever. Cries of pain and despair find their places in dreams that will not leave you alone. Where would they put me on this ship? Would I be locked in a cage? There was nothing to do but take the next step.

Dumas looked at me oddly when he saw me the next morning standing on the dock wearing my same rags with nothing in my hands. I had been waiting for almost an hour, well before the appointed time.

"No other clothes, Dr. P? I didn't think of that, but not to worry. I have an extra blouse and britches that will cover you until we make St. Croix. We might even put you in a pair of shoes. Follow me." He tossed his canvas bag to me for me to carry.

I just nodded my head. Nervous and determined not to do or say anything at this critical time of departure that might upset anyone in anyway, I was sweating like I was bent over in the fields. I clutched his bag glad to have something to hold onto. We stepped off the dock down into a waiting boat where three or four seamen were already seated. Two oarsmen were onboard ready to row us to the schooner anchored a short distance out in the harbor. As we approached the ship I felt numb. The excitement of leaving and the fear of boarding a ship swirled within me until I felt I would puke. Reaching the ship, everyone took a turn climbing aboard leaving me, the slave, last to come up. Nicolas helped me onto the deck and casually led me down to the first level below deck. Crammed into the forward starboard corner was a small space barely large enough for the hammock that hung within.

"You will bunk here when you are not at work on deck, Dr. P," Nicolas explained. I stared at the hammock and stared back at Dumas. The most elaborate captain's quarters on one of the largest ships in the world could not have made a greater impression on me. Yes, I was still the slave but on this ship I was actually provided a place to rest. I would be fed the same food that the sailors ate. Much of the fear that gripped me began to fade away although I was still nervous, far from feeling comfortable once again being onboard a ship. Nicolas sensed my fear. He turned to me,

"Dr. P, you are owned by Monsieur Royer. Royer owns this ship and the sugar down in the hold. You are here with me and we have a job to do for Royer. No one here will cause us trouble. Do what I tell you to do. That is your only concern."

"Oui, monsieur. The ship that brought me here to Saint Domingue was much different. Were you brought here on a ship, Dumas?" I asked.

Nicolas stepped back and looked at me closely. After a pause I was surprised as he pulled his loose fitting shirt over his head. Handing me the shirt, with his brown chest glistening from perspiration reflected in the dim light, he instructed me to put it on. I did as I was told. Dumas then explained,

"No, Dr. P. I was born here, a Creole native. It was my father, a seaman from Lisbon, who came by ship. My mother was a native. When I was ten they both died from malaria and I was on my own. Trying to keep from starving, I worked in the fields, on the docks – I worked around every type of slave here in Saint Domingue. At twelve, I was kidnapped from the fields by two men who took me to the far end of the island where I was illegally sold as a slave bound for Cuba. It is a long story but I escaped before the ship left Saint Domingue. There is a record of my birth, a free birth, here in this town. I have worked for the Royer plantation often over the years. In addition to working as a seaman on Royer ships I have also shipped out with a Portuguese trader who knew my father. Like you, speaking French has been important but I can read and write the French as well. This is key. It was the written record that saved me. I trust no stranger. I carry my reminder confirming the foulness of men with me everywhere."

Slowly Dumas turned his back to me. Old scars from a large whip covered his back. The twelve year old boy had escaped his slave ship, but the beating he received before reclaiming freedom must have been as brutal as any I had ever seen. There was nothing for me to say. He turned back to me and shrugged,

"Do what I tell you to do. No one will give you trouble here." Nicolas Dumas picked up his canvas bag and walked away to his own berth.

Over the next four days I was busy from dawn to dusk, mainly scrubbing decks and moving sacks of sugar. It was strange to be on a ship and actually work on assigned tasks, even such low tasks as scrubbing the deck. I would always be nervous on a ship. For me, they never seemed safe and the constant roll of the sea never felt right. But I was part of the group working to get the ship to St. Croix and I earned my meals each day. The hammock in the tiny forward berth seemed a luxury and I slept hard each night. I kept my head down, my mouth shut and welcomed any direction Nicolas gave me. It seemed to me that he actually liked me and that we might have become friends had we spent any time together. Perhaps I just wanted to feel that way. It had been wise on my part to speak up the way I did when Dumas and Pascal were talking on the Port Au Prince docks but it was Nicolas who had actually made all this happen for me.

We rode a favorable wind and by noon on the fifth day we entered the harbor of Christiansted on the island of St. Croix. Part of what they called the Danish West Indies, a country of people named Denmark with a flag of red and white was the one who owned St. Croix. The white men from France owned the island of Saint Domingue. Sailing to the east from Saint Domingue, we had passed the island which men from Spain called Puerto Rico. Back behind us to the west was the large island that the Spaniards called Cuba. All of these islands where brown people lived is where the white men with the ships from France, England, Spain and Denmark moved the black people like me from Africa to grow the sugarcane. These different countries were still strange to me but as I was being traded and moved around their islands I began to understand. The people who had ships and cannon took over the places where the sugarcane was grown. Taking the islands was not enough. To get more sugar they needed to get more men to cut the 'cane. More sugar, more men, more dead, more men, more sugar and it seemed there was never enough.

As our schooner was secured dockside I would have been scrubbing decks and helping get cargo ready to unload but Dumas ordered me to follow him off the ship. It was early afternoon and a few dark clouds were beginning to gather off to the east signaling a late afternoon shower heading our way. The streets of Christiansted going west away from the docks are called Queen Street, King Street and Company Street. The busy street going north to south crossing over the others is Kings Crossing. Nicolas walked the four blocks quickly and we stood in front of the counting house called Beekman and C ruger on the northwest corner of King and Kings C rossing S treets. I waited outside as Nicolas went in to find the manager. J ust as quickl y he came back out having been told that the manager was a few blocks away tending to some business at the C ustoms House. Nicolas glanced at me and shrugged,

"We have some time to wait. Let's try to find something to eat."

Slowly a mule pulling a cart half full of mangos and bananas passed us and headed over two blocks to Company Street. The man tending the mule stopped where another man and a woman, both black and both wearing large brimmed straw hats, sat on a short bench under a canopy that provided shade to their vegetable and fruit stand. The two men conducted some business while the woman waited on Nicolas who paid her for some fruit. As we sat and ate watching the people of Christiansted come and go, I tried to think about what might happen next. Only weeks earlier, if any of us in the fields could get our hands on fresh fruit we would be hoarding it worrying that it might be taken from us. Now, I was not only away from the plantation, I was gone from Saint Domingue altogether sitting casually on a street corner in Christiansted, St. Croix! My companion was a free Creole. I walked the streets with him as if I was almost a free man myself. Part of my brain screamed to me to try and look for some way to escape. The other part of me understood that Nicolas Dumas was the only free man with some authority who had paid any attention to me at all over the past eight years. True, Dumas did not own me and true, Dumas could not free me but over the past ten days this man had helped turn my world around. It was hard to imagine what might come next and harder still to try and stay calm but, for now, it made sense to stay close to Dumas and to seek his advice.

Within the hour we were back at Beekman and Cruger's office. Nicolas needed to know the schedule for the arrival of the six slaves due in from Cuba. When the slaves reached St. Croix it was Dumas who would have coordinated their delivery with the captain of the Royer schooner so all hands would be prepared to set sail for Port Au Prince without delay. Nicolas was told that the office manager had returned from Custom House. The youngster who came forward introduced himself as Alexander Hamilton and explained to Dumas that their ship from Cuba was expected within three to four days due to foul weather. It seemed that prevailing winds, normally out of the west, had been reversed as the odd storm from the east was upon us. The ship due in from Cuba, well west of St. Croix, would have normally been riding favorable winds. Now she was sailing into head winds. The delivery of the slaves was at least three days out. Master Hamilton and Dumas came out of the office onto King Street to more closely monitor the direction and strength of the wind. The young Hamilton noticed me as I had been waiting outside. Dumas turned and made the introduction with a flourish;

"Master Hamilton, this is my man brought from Saint-Domingue to assist me in the management of these new Royer slaves. May I present Prince, or the honorable Dr. P as I am inclined to call him."

With a slight smile Hamilton nodded to me, " Bon après-midi, monsieur Prince et bienvenue dans notre île de Saint-Croix … Good afternoon, mister Prince, and welcome to our island of Saint Croix."

Looking him in the eye, I quickly spoke up, "Je suis honoré Maître Hamilton. Et puis-je vous féliciter, pour être sélectionné comme directeur de cette maison de comptage respectée tout en étant encore si tôt dans vos années …I am honored Master Hamilton. And may I please offer congratulations to you, sir, to be selected as manager of this respected counting house while still so early in your years."

My response caught him by surprise and he eyed me more closely. "Your French is well spoken, Mr. Prince, and I appreciate the compliment. Have you and Mr. Dumas worked together long?"

Bowing slightly, I replied, "You honor me, sir. Please understand, I am but a slave to the Royer family and Mr. Dumas was kind enough to have me assigned to assist him on this voyage."

Now Dumas turned to Hamilton and gave him some background, "At an early age Prince was taught the French by his father, the leader of a Dahomey tribe. He is not your average slave, Master Hamilton."

"I can see that he is not. Prince, we must speak again before it is time for you to depart Saint Croix", was this young man's kind response.

I nodded again and began to follow Dumas back to the ship. My head was swimming. Nicolas treated me like a man and this young counting house clerk had said he looked forward to speaking with me? It was like rain in the desert. I could not make sense of it all but the voice inside me kept putting the word "calm" in front of me. Nicolas seemed to keep calm most all the time so I tried to mimic his behavior.

The next three days were overcast and steady rain gave the island a good soaking. It was just a routine stretch of rainy weather but the slower pace around Christiansted allowed me extra time to follow along with Dumas. With little else to do, we checked in with Hamilton and the clerks at Beekman and Cruger twice a day. It was on the second day with a pelting rain gusting over the docks that we hurried into the offices and I first saw the man who would prove that my miserable luck could actually change for the better.

In Liverpool the crew of the *Nelly* had reported as directed by Captain Christopher and returned to sea with basically the same men as on their two prior trips stretching over the past two years. Two, maybe three, new crew had joined a seasoned group that had come to learn and understand the risks and reward that defined the slave trade. For Billy Simms the organization and camaraderie of the *Nelly* was a welcome relief from the family in turmoil that he left behind.

By the spring of 1772 Gutle and Mayer Amschel Rothschild were moving forward starting a family as Gutle had given birth to their first child. The confines of Frankfurt's Judengasse would not hold her sons and their ambitions to unite the capitals of Europe in a banking empire but Gutle would always prefer to remain close to the Judengasse. The Rothschild name and reputation would become highly visible across the continent but when major accomplishes were celebrated, Gutle brought her family and their focus back to Frankfurt and the Judengasse. Other cities might one day be central to the family fortune but the Judengasse would forever hold Gutle's heart.

PRINCE of SAND - Chapter Eight ... Traverser la ligne / Crossing the Line

The African coast lay low on the eastern horizon as dawn emerged on a cold November morning. Captain Christopher, with the *Nelly* three days out from Annamaboe, was anticipating yet another negotiating session with Jaja and Nimba. With his reach deep into the interior of the continent Jaja was now widely recognized as the largest kidnapper operating on the Gold Coast. He and his chief lieutenant, the warrior Nimba, controlled a chain of suppliers who brought members of weaker tribes off of the plains and down from the highlands in numbers unmatched by any other single slave broker. Captain C returned to Annamaboe time and again not because the prices were cheap. No, Jaja would never be described as the least expensive of the slave makers. The single feature that distinguished Jaja from the others was the strength of his supply chain. No one could quite understand how Nimba organized and maintained order over the small army of soldiers that he directed in the field but he and Jaja could arrange the capture of large groups of humans and load them into the holds of outward-bound vessels with dependable regularity. It was the time saved in loading the *Nelly* and the knowledge that the product stored below would bring decent prices in South America that kept Captain C coming back. Billy Simms and the crew had come to appreciate the relatively quick turnaround in unloading cargo and filling the *Nelly* with African captives. Stories from other ships who spent months trying to gather a crop of captives by moving down the coast picking up small groups of slaves at a time were frightening. Seldom were slaves successful in organizing meaningful resistance against the sailors that forced them below but that did not keep them from trying. Some were determined to fight for their shattered lives. The longer the anger and despair simmered below deck the more likely a furious young warrior might try to drive a sharp object into the neck of an unsuspecting member of the crew. For Billy, such stories caused him to grip his whip that much tighter while keeping a vigilant eye on every black son-of-a-bitch that fouled the *Nelly's* deck. Beat the hell out of anyone who even thought about making eye contact, much less made a threatening move. Give any asshole onboard good reason to pause before he fucked with Billy Simms. That was the plan and Simms had come safely through every situation he had faced. For Billy Simms, he would stick to his one tried and true survival plan - to beat the piss out of every slave in sight.

While comfortable with his place onboard the Nelly and going to sea serving Captain C, Billy was more alone on this first leg of the slaver expedition than ever before. Always the loner, he was now almost invisible to the rest of the crew. No one would ever know that his last two nights in Liverpool had turned even the detached Simms inside out. For years he had brought his whip out from under the bed whenever his mood suited him and Janet had learned how to survive these bizarre displays of anger. Careful not to bruise areas normally exposed to others, Billy gave vent to a twisted and deeply centered frustration.

Simms became angry and often violent toward anyone he judged to be weak or inferior to himself. Somewhere in the back of his mind early memories from the hated orphanage haunted and shaped Billy Simms. Memories so vivid, so frightening that he would not even try to sleep when terror from his youth flooded his thoughts. No one, not even Janet, knew that by the time he was six years old Billy Simms had often seen death take it's toll among the other children, a few dying practically in his arms. The winter of 1750 had brought on an onslaught of contagious disease that shook the entire west coast of England. Men and women of all ages suffered everything from measles and chicken pox to cholera and the flu. It was the children and the elderly who were struck down in startling numbers. No one understood that fleas and lice rampant among rats that thrived around the Liverpool docks proved to be a remarkably efficient colony for many strains of deadly disease. Billy was just a little boy who knew nothing about disease. His brutal introduction came firsthand when he became violently ill suffering from both chicken pox and then cholera as a six year old.

It seemed that no child in the orphanage was spared as the overwhelmed staff tried to keep the sick children separated from others. Still the high fevers and deadly flu symptoms took their toll. One bitterly cold night, almost delirious with fever, Billy would recall that he and a five year old, Chad Watson, had been placed side-by-side in a bed as they were both suffering the same symptoms. Sometime in the last hours before dawn Billy's fever broke. He awoke around six a.m. in a pool of sweat. Pitifully weak but feeling like he was back in his own head, his eyes no longer felt like they were on fire. The blanket that covered him felt like it must weigh six hundred pounds. He stretched and his left leg brushed up against his bedmate. He was relieved to recall that he was not in hospital alone. Without raising his head from the pillow, Billy looked to his left to see if Chad Watson was also awake. The little boy's eyes were wide open and their noses practically touched but the Watson child, his mouth slightly ajar, was no longer awake. Startled to be staring into a pair of unblinking eyes, Billy instinctively put out his left hand as if to keep something away. It was the dead boy's grey-white complexion and the cold touch of death that locked themselves together in Billy's mind for the rest of his days. Slowly, without making a sound, Billy rolled over onto his right shoulder turning his back to the corpse next to him and faced the wall. When an exhausted member of the staff eventually made rounds and pulled the dead child from the bed she found Billy shaking, slightly curled up close to the wall. The Simms child was whimpering. Billy seldom cried but this was different. Young Billy Simms was scared.

Throughout his years, Billy's response to weakness was to punish it in some way. Something switched on in his brain when he physically expressed dominance over someone he could control. Most often it made no difference to anyone but his victim. But two nights before shipping out on this expedition even Simms realized that he had crossed a line – a line that mattered. Janet was working late hours at the tavern while Billy had spent his evening in cups of rum with some of the crew as they traded old stories and shared their enthusiasm for going back to sea. Simms was in a drunken haze when he returned home and climbed the narrow staircase. Calling out for Janet, he heard nothing. Frustrated, he loudly cursed as he stumbled against their single chair,

"Fuck this bloody shit hole and fuck that bitch for leaving me to a cold bed!"

From the other room he heard a short gasp. Two steps to his left and he shoved open the door to see his daughter in bed, her cover pulled round her chin.

"Where be your brother and what be in this house for a man to eat?"

Nancy stared at him and did not open her mouth. Her brother Peter stayed away from these two rooms as much as he could and, even drunk, Billy knew that only a couple of stale biscuits were gathering mold in an otherwise empty cupboard.

Screaming now in rising anger, Simms made his demands, "Speak when I bloody well ask you something you little shit!"

Nancy stared at the little man, mocking him with her silence. Shaking with rage, Billy turned on his heel and went to his bed. Down on his knees, he reached under the bed and brought out his small sack. As any child that age, particularly one living in such a cramped space, ten year-old Nancy knew everything about what was stored under that bed. Children paid attention to such things and anyone paying attention to Nancy realized she was already beginning to take on the shape of a woman. Two months from turning eleven, she would soon surpass her mother's striking good looks as she grew into her teenage years.

Billy walked back in the doorway. Nancy saw something familiar and also something she had never seen before. Billy held the whip firmly in his fist. That whip, the one with a red strand of leather laced into the handle, was well known to both Nancy and to her brother. She had seen the whip many times before but this was the first time she had ever seen a grown man standing before her without any clothes. Her brain told her it was too late to say anything at all.

The *Nelly* would soon be out to sea and Billy would desperately hope that the tonic of being outward bound would take his mind away from his last days in Liverpool but his foul crimes denied him peace of mind. Janet had quietly slipped into bed arriving just over an hour after Billy had finished wreaking terror upon their youngest child.

Only father and daughter would ever know the full extent of what had taken place but those two rooms could not keep silent such an unspeakable episode. Like a wharf rat scurrying to hide in a dark place, Simms had slipped out of bed, down the stairs and out into the mist before anyone else stirred that morning. Thick fog sitting low on the docks served as a shroud as he walked quickly toward the *Nelly*.

Crew and workers loading cargo from the warehouses would be crawling over the ship all day making her ready for sea and the first leg to Annamaboe. Billy arrived speaking to no one and straight away climbed high into the rigging. Starting in the bow beginning with the foremast he made certain all sails were properly furled and ready to be set upon Captain Christopher's commands. From this perch he kept an eye on those approaching and boarding the deck of his home at sea. In the back of his mind he could picture Janet half dragging the constable down to the wharf demanding that Billy be taken from the ship and slapped into irons. He would be rudely accused of unnatural acts and roundly scorned by the only real family he understood, his mates aboard the *Nelly*. Preparing the *Nelly* to depart Liverpool was normally a joy. This day seemed to have no end. Finally, near dusk, he correctly surmised that no one was coming for him. Now he was forced to make his decision. Would he return to those two rooms as if nothing had happened or hole up onboard the *Nelly* and fade away on the morning tide while trying to put all this shit behind him? He had been weighing his options throughout the day. Waiting and half expecting to be accused at any moment over a full day had been miserable. The thought of being at sea for the better part of a year with only his imagination to shape the steps toward his demise that Janet might be taking seemed worse to Billy than the dread he felt about going back up those stairs. Climbing down from the mizzenmast in the stern of the ship, he wasted no time and began the short walk home.

Billy was back onboard the Nelly well before dawn with his small bag of gear stored in the small berth aft and starboard that he now shared with the cook. In the darkness before dawn with his bag thrown over his shoulder no one noticed a faint vertical line of blood between his shoulder blades that had seeped onto his tan shirt. At home, Billy had opened the door and climbed the creaking staircase with the same determined gait that had carried him back from the ship. Only as he reached to open the door at the top of the stairs did he pause, listening to try and learn something from within. Hearing nothing, he slowly pushed on the door and stepped inside. Now he heard swift motion behind him. Pain exploded across his shoulders before he could turn. Wincing and stumbling onto his right knee, he twisted to his left looking for his attacker. Billy saw Janet, her hands high above her head as she brought an iron poker down toward him with all of her strength. Her hair was matted and wild across her face. Enraged eyes bulged from their sockets as spittle flew from her lips. Every fiber within tried to bring pain onto the man who had been beating her for years. He successfully deflected the blow with his left forearm and backhanded his wife across the face with a blow that would have stopped large men in their tracks. Physically, Janet did not cause Billy any real concern. The veteran of bar room scrapes and brawls with enraged slaves was not going to be taken down by a woman. But it was the look of a protective and threatened mother that was intimidating and fearful. For hours Janet had been waiting, sitting in the chair while holding the poker she had scrounged. Nancy, in shock and numb in her confusion, had remained in bed all morning unwilling or unable to speak about what had taken place. But Janet knew. She knew her husband. She knew all she needed to know. After gathering Nancy up and moving her to rooms above the tavern, the wounded mother had returned to sit by the door praying for the bastard to return. Her mind was blank and oddly calm as she waited, her ear trained to the bottom step before Billy finally began to climb.

Janet, only momentarily dazed by the pain from his blow, came at him from a crouch using her two hands to try and rip his eyes from his head. With Janet scratching and kicking, Billy stumbled to the edge of the bed to grab his small sack. He shoved her back into the other room and bounded down the stairs. Not a single word had been uttered between the two. Within the hour Simms lay curled up in his hammock aboard the *Nelly*. He was in his safe place but sleep refused to join him there. He was learning. The line that was crossed, a line running straight and true for as long as the eye could see, had stood between Billy and a place from which there was no escape. Slightly curled on his side, his face inches from the bulkhead, Billy Simms was scared.

On the other side of the Channel working his way through the crowded Frankfurt streets, Amschel Mayer Rothschild tightly held onto his father's hand. Gutle's second child and oldest son had spent a glorious day with his father moving from one shop or business to another. Amschel gazed at his father as he gestured and spoke with purpose to different friends. Proudly Mayer Rothschild introduced his boy to these men, laughing and referring to young Amschel as his 'Nummer Eins Chef' - his Number One Boss. The youngster did not recognize anyone or pretend to understand what all the fuss was about, only that he was on an adventure with Papa! The sounds and smells of Frankfurt mesmerized the child. Papa led him to his favorite bakery where the luxurious aroma of fresh streuselkuchen being taken from the oven enveloped him. The delicious pastry was as warm as the smile behind Papa's whiskers. Many of Amschel Mayer Rothschild's earliest memories would be formed this day. Together, happy and exhausted, father and son passed through one of the three gates exiting the inner city back to their home. Still holding hands, the two crossed over and back into the Judengasse, their familiar village within the city, both eager to tell Mama all about their day in Frankfurt.

Across the Atlantic, two days out from Saint Croix, the ship from Cuba carrying the new slaves who would be taken by Nicolas Dumas to their new owner on Saint-Domingue was making her way to Christiansted. Young Alexander Hamilton had expressed interest in speaking with me further after our brief exchange when he understood that we both spoke the French. To my delight and surprise, we did indeed have the opportunity to have our conversation when he invited me into the offices during one of Dumas' visits to Beekman and C ruger . Quickly we realized that both of us had been separated from our parents as teenagers. Hamilton's mother had died a few years earlier long after his father had deserted them and he was genuinely interested to learn how I had come to be kidnapped and sold. We both shared an ability to understand more than one language but there our similarities abruptly stopped. Once again, as when I first met Dumas, my instinct was to speak up and trust a stranger with the desperate hope that reward might outweigh risk. As directly as I could speak, I told Hamilton that being permitted to leave Saint-Domingue under the supervision of Dumas was the single most hopeful event that had happened for me over the past ten years. Looking him in the eye, I said that only death would befriend me back on that island from hell. My left hand I lay on the desk as I explained how I crippled myself to escape cutting the sugarcane. Alexander stared at me intently and glanced at my hand. Quietly he asked,

"Prince, you now wish to find another means of leaving Christiansted?"

Without blinking I held his gaze and slowly nodded my head.

After a full minute Hamilton broke the silence, "It would be useless to try and escape on another ship. This is a small port. Vessels arriving and departing are well documented. The captains of the ships are well known and within the reach of trade officials. You belong to the Royer family and their interests would be protected. The delivery of Royer slaves will occur any day now sending you with Dumas back to your predicament. I see only one alternative that might improve your state."

Staring at him I lightly shrugged my shoulders and asked, "And what is this alternative of which you speak?"

Alexander had now turned his head and gazed out of the window. Speaking softly he explained, "There is a ship here that will set sail for the colonies in three days, bound for Charleston." Turning back to face me, he continued, "If it was possible for you to be sold once again, there is an agent here from Charleston representing the interests of the Horry family and their sizable rice plantations in the place known as the Low Country of carolina. Yes, you are a slave in Saint-Domingue and you would simply become a slave in the low country. But perhaps, in the end, this would be a good trade for you. The coast of the colonies is enormous. My instinct is that your chances to improve yourself would be more plentiful to the north. Were I in your place, I would try to move in that direction."

While the thought of being sold yet again weighed heavy on my mind, it only took me a moment to conclude that finding any way out of Saint-Domingue was the first objective. And time was not on my side. "Please, Master Hamilton, do you think you can bring about such a sale?"

Now Hamilton furrowed his brow and slightly shook his head. "Prince, you will know more about that than me. I am a clerk for a trading house. We work to help traders make successful transactions but we are not buyers or sellers. The question, Mr. Prince, is can your Mr. Dumas offer you for sale and will he consider such a course of action?"

The Creole from Saint-Domingue soon joined us. These two, one of whom was almost young enough to be my son, could make or break the opportunity that might be mine. As Nicolas took a seat next to me I was prepared to bluntly ask for his help. Alexander looked over and raised his palm to me before I could begin. He calmly began, "Prince, thank you for your suggestions. May I ask that you take some time to stretch your legs while Mr. Dumas and I discuss a few business matters?"

He nodded toward the door and I nodded in return. Standing, I met his eyes and bowed slightly. As I walked out onto King Street, instinctively heading toward the docks, a stream of emotions ran through me. Hope, frustration, excitement, anger – the mix was confusing. My very existence was on the table for discussion and yet here I was strolling along the street with nowhere to go. But relief was also part of what I felt. Arranging such a transaction was nothing I was ever allowed to take part in, other than serving as the piece of meat being sold on the block. This youngster, Hamilton, was a trader. If he could possibly make a seller of Dumas and find a buyer from this

Charleston place, for the first time I would happily step forward as the "meat on the block". What choice did I have? My choices had evaporated to nothing when a net was dropped on me in the forest at home. Home? Just the thought of having a home was strange and had been now for years. It is a very sad thing to think about, this not having a home. Ask me about choices and I will ask you to shake my left hand.

It may have been a few minutes later, it may have been an hour – I honestly cannot recall and such details were far from my mind – but Dumas stepped out to the street and gestured for me to return. I walked in where the two of them were sitting at the desk, their expressions telling me nothing. Nicolas began to speak as I was taking a seat, "Prince, Mr. Hamilton has suggested that I consider a trade. There is an agent from the colony of Charleston here in Christiansted trading for his client's account. In addition to freight being loaded for shipment this agent might be interested to learn if skilled slaves are available for purchase. If a large price can be gained, I would return to Port-Au-Prince having earned Mr. Royer's continued support as he much prefers handsome profit over one extra nigger. However, if I was to return without you after making a poor trade, I would be held directly responsible for making payments to Royer that I cannot afford. You need to understand. I will not and cannot be selling anything that belongs to Mr. Royer unless the bag of coins I will carry back to Saint-Domingue is heavy, indeed." Looking over to Hamilton, Dumas shrugged, "Alexander, now Prince and I must return to assist in preparations for our return to Port-Au-Prince. Please let me know if your agent friend would like to look Prince over."

My dream that night was long and colorful even though I never closed my eyes. Of course, I had no idea what this place called Charleston looked like or how long the journey to something called Low Country might take but I saw myself there just the same. Vordun could be sending me a blessing or Hades, Prince of the Darkness, might be calling me to his trap but I wanted to see this Charleston and hoped to roam among the colonies. My heart raced when Dumas called on me the next morning to join him. It seemed Hamilton's trader friend from Charleston wanted to see me. Within minutes I was on my way to meet Mr. Barnwell - James Thomas Barnwell, proudly hailing from the harbor where they say that the Ashley and Cooper Rivers come together as one to form the Atlantic Ocean! It would be a lie if I said I was not nervous as we went one last time to the Beekman and Cruger office. No one needed to explain to me that perhaps the only chance for me to forever leave the sugarcane behind was now upon me. I waited on the street as Dumas stepped inside looking for Master Hamilton. Almost immediately he came back out asking me to come inside. Hamilton stood and, speaking in the English, turned to the slender white man with dark hair seated next to him;

"Mr. Barnwell, this is the man named Prince from the plains of Dahomey."

I did not know much of the English but it was clear what the talk was about as this scene was very familiar to me. Once again, I was being measured for sale. This man named Barnwell looked at me and then he would speak the English. Young Hamilton listened and would then speak the French to Dumas,

"Mr. Barnwell asks to have Prince talk about going to the America. He wishes to hear him speak in the French."

Dumas nodded and simply turned to me awaiting my response,

"Mon temps dans la canne a sucre a ete tres difficile" … "My time in the sugarcane has been very hard" … "I am still a young man with many years remaining to work for my master. I believe I will live to work longer if I can move north to the colonies."

Beatings from the seaman Simms and others had taught me to look straight ahead or down at my feet. This Jamie Barnwell stood close to me causing me to look him in the eye. He asked a question in a quiet voice. Hamilton spoke to me,

"He asks that you explain what happened to your hand."

"I was taught the different steps to make the sugar from the 'cane. My hand was crushed in an accident at the mill where the 'cane is pressed" was my measured response.

"Please tell Mr. Barnwell if you were trained for any other work."

I looked at Jamie Barnwell as I answered Hamilton, "The fields of 'cane are fed water from the large river by a system of canals and ditches which control the flow of the water. I have been taught where the ditches must be dug and how to help fix where the water goes."

Something I said caused Barnwell to quickly look from Hamilton to Dumas and back to me. Now Hamilton spoke quietly to Dumas,

"Please, Nicolas, if you and Prince can give us a few minutes, Mr. Barnwell and I have some business to discuss further."

Dumas and I stood just outside the large white shutters that were propped open in the two windows of the front office. The subtle fragrance from a flowering bush hung in the heavy air. It was not long before Dumas was called back to the table. My future tumbled back and forth across the room as the Saint-Domingue Creole and the white man from Charleston played out the hand with the young orphan from St. Croix serving as the gate-keeper.

Mr. Barnwell shook his head, "Yes, I can tell that he knows the French. And yes, my client must control the flooding of his Ashley River rice fields to keep his plantation both operating and growing. To own a French speaking slave who is trained in the irrigation of the rice fields is something my client will be interested in. But damn-it, Alexander, the price is just too high to pay for a slave missing half of his left hand!"

Dumas listened to Hamilton with raised eyes and shaking his head he said, "I know, Alexander, that you understand my situation. Mr. Royer awaits six new slaves who will be accompanied by me and his older slave, Prince. Prince will be with me or I will hand over to Mr. Royer the large number of gold coins that I must have to explain his absence."

"And you cannot move from your price?" asked Alexander.

Dumas just shrugged.

Now Hamilton and Barnwell spoke in a whisper, their mouths to each other's ear. Jamie Barnwell then moved back from Alexander and simply nodded his head. And it was done. The next ship that I would board would set sail for Charleston three days hence!

One of Hamilton's clerks brought over a piece of paper for Barnwell and Dumas to sign. It would be years before I learned how Alexander had brought the two together. The Charleston trading house of Begbie and Barnwell had maintained accounts with Beekman and Cruger over many years. Young Hamilton had simply taken a long-term perspective regarding this trade. Shaping something agreeable for Mr. Barnwell made sense and Hamilton had a gift for closing a deal. Hamilton had whispered to Barnwell that the ten percent fee earned by Beekman and Cruger and paid by the seller for this transaction would be credited to Begbie and Barnwell's account. Now Barnwell had room to pass an acceptable price on to his client. Hamilton handled this trade for free, giving up his fee to get what he wanted out of the deal. He wanted to see me on a ship sailing north to Charleston. Do not ask me because I cannot tell you why. It has always been a mystery to me that he would give a rat's ass as to where I would be sailing when I left Christiansted.

The Saint-Domingue Creole bearing scars from the harsh end of a whip had pushed the limit of his authority by offering me for sale. This white man from the colonies named Jamie had agreed to pay 'full price' for the slave missing half of his left hand. The youngster behind the desk had made it his mission to bring buyer and seller together. These men had lifted me up and carried me over a line that was impossible for me to cross alone. After years of isolation I would be returning to something closer to living. Still a slave, my condition was both unnatural and unacceptable, but at least for now a few people seemed to give a shit. All of this had happened quickly in 1772.

Perhaps an extra bowl of chicken blood had been sacrificed and offered to vordun. Maybe the jesus so many called out to had smiled when a large group of his christ people had gathered to practice drinking his blood. It did not matter to me as my eyes were now turned north to those colonies in the place called North America. The next day I cleared my berth from the Royer schooner as Dumas loaded the six new slaves who would return with him to their new hell in Royer's sugarcane. As I was leaving the ship, Dumas called out to me. I turned as he walked up, placed one hand on my shoulder and handed me a small canvas bag with the other. Four words passed his lips as he wished me good luck,

"Bonne chance, monsieur Prince."

Nicolas was rubbing his eye as he turned and walked away. I looked down into my bag. Two clean shirts and a new pair of trousers were tucked inside. My name is Prince although my mother always called me Yamar, the name she had given me. And my wealth had just greatly increased.

PRINCE of SAND - Chapter Nine – Nouveaux Points sur la Carte / New Points on the Map

Nancy's mother had talked to her a few times about the return of the *Nelly*. To her credit, Janet was determined to keep the fear Nancy must have for that man, her father, from defining her daughter's life. Often, caught up in her anger toward Billy, Janet was consumed with her own guilt for leaving both Nancy and Peter to bear witness to their father's beastly habits year after year after year. Some family traditions defined the golden years for a youngster's storybook childhood. Other repeated behaviors would never be acknowledged. How is it that something so large, so overwhelming is never mentioned? Perhaps it never happened.

The biting cold of December and January had come and gone as Liverpool huddled under the grey skies of February. Nancy and Peter had learned from Janet that the Nelly was reported to be three weeks out with her arrival expected during the first week of March. Yes, they dreaded his return but Nancy always felt happy about the arrival of March. There was no denying that storms in March could match the most brutal winter weather. That was true. But it was also a given that March would give way to spring. Simply the thought of spring brought a smile to the remarkable Nancy Simms. With every reason to be sullen and withdrawn, she moved with confidence and focus. Janet was now as much a sister as mother to Nancy as the child began to mature beyond her years. Each thrived in the relationship and their friendship helped prevent both from being trapped in the suffocating loneliness that was Billy Simms in this new year of 1773.

So the weeks slipped by and the day had arrived. On a morning that was both crisp and clear without a cloud in sight, the three, Janet, Peter and Nancy, had "cleared the deck" as two spotless rooms were ready for his arrival. Mechanically they moved toward the docks recalling the tavern gossip of certain crew rumored to have perished on the voyage. It was always the case that such stories would circulate until later when both Captain Christopher and Billy would explain what had actually taken place. Who had been weak in the face of illness? Did someone fail to pay attention to a savage slave? Perhaps one of the men from the *Nelly* had crossed the wrong sailor in a dark alley of some port in Brazil. As was their custom on the *Nelly*, Helmsman Olson stood at the top of the gangway to read the list of the dead prior to the crew being released for liberty. Janet and the children gazed about, acknowledging a few familiar faces. By now Janet could name most of the crew and she pointed out some of the men to Peter as she scanned the ship for Billy. Mr. Olson was reading the last two names,

" … Third Mate Jacque Ferrier … and Seaman First Class Billy Simms."

Olson folded his piece of paper and turned to continue with his other duties. Janet was certain she had heard him say "Seaman First Class Billy Simms" but it had not begun to dawn on her that her husband had perished on this expedition. Billy was dead? The man who loved to go to sea aboard the *Nelly* more than anything else in the world had not made it back to Liverpool? Now she gasped loudly and grabbed the arms of her two children, each next to her on either side. Peter placed his hand over hers and turned to face to his Mother. Nancy did not move. Her face betrayed no emotion but her pulse was racing. In that moment everything seemed to slow down. Images and colors became sharply focused. Staring out to sea, her gaze was drawn to a large flock of over one hundred blackbirds flying from Nancy's left to her right directly into the face of a brisk ten-knot breeze. The flock, moving as one, worked hard to travel a short distance going up against the wind. Then the entire group seemed to stall, gathering closer together and rising higher as the wind pushed them back. Nancy shielded her eyes from a bright morning sun sparkling across the water. Suddenly, in the blink of an eye, every bird folded their left wing to their side and, as if following a silent command, dropped their heads slightly toward the docks as they turned away from the wind. Now reversed and riding the wind toward the western horizon, the flock exploded forward with remarkable speed. Before you could repeat the name 'Seaman Billy Simms', the entire flock had sped down along the waterfront, now almost out of sight.

Twelve years of age is too young to truly grasp one's destiny. Youngsters cannot be expected to see much beyond the four walls of a schoolroom. But there are moments when your life changes. Bitter tragedy can explode from within leaving you struggling just to place one foot in front of the other. Or the change might be welcome. In a heartbeat, in a split second with no warning or hint as to what is taking place, such a moment can come over you like a new layer of skin. Nancy now watched her life begin to take shape for the first time. She could sense that her future was brighter even if she would be hard pressed to explain how. Obstacles that she could not begin to measure or manage on her own were eliminated when the helmsman, Mr. Olson, read names from a piece of paper. Questions so difficult to form, much less answer, had simply died with that man, her father. Nancy felt no sorrow nor took pleasure at the news. She was just hugely relieved. Now she turned to her Mother and wondered. Now they were three when last night, in their minds, they had been four. These three looked at one another as they came together to embrace as one. The sun was on their faces. The awkward stress of preparing to greet the undesired guest was lifted from their brow. Truly, this family was now in a safer place than before which only the three of them could truly begin to understand.

So what had actually happened to Billy Simms? Condolences were being offered to Janet by two or three of the crew when she looked up and saw Captain Christopher striding toward her. After dismissing the crew, the Captain had looked for Janet as he came down the gangway and onto the docks. Now he spoke to her in a hushed voice,

"Mrs. Simms, my heart is sad over your loss which must come to you so hard here today. The *Nelly* lost her most dedicated seaman when Billy Simms died. He will be missed."

Janet nodded her head slightly and made certain not to smile. "Please, Captain, can you tell me how it happened?"

Peter wondered if his father had been swept from the rigging, high up on the mast, while trying to take in sail during a violent storm. Janet half expected to hear that her husband had been stabbed to death in some dark alley after spending the night in a tub of rum, his pockets empty when they found him. Nancy was numb. She was just listening to the words being spoken around her.

The good Captain C shrugged slightly and spoke in a solemn tone, "We were two days out of Annamaboe when fever spread among both crew and the cargo below. Most just fought through the fever, weak but still alive to speak of it. Mr. Simms also suffered greatly from his loose bowels. His fever could not be contained. Delirious, he clung hard to the edge of a bunk and called for us to remove a dead child from his bed, clearly out of his head with the fever. We placed a fresh set of leeches upon him to be rid of the bad blood but he had lost all strength from the run of his bowels and passed in the early morning of the sixth day. He was buried at sea with all hands on deck on November 14, 1772. That costly fever claimed two of my crew and eight trade units from below the deck. You have my sympathy, Mrs. Simms."

Janet could hardly believe her ears. Billy Simms, a man born to sail the seven seas, had shit himself to death! The fever and diarrhea had struck early in November and he was dead within a matter of days. It did not seem possible but Billy had been dead for almost four full months. Slipped over the side of the ship, he was no doubt met promptly by sharks trailing the *Nelly* looking for just such an offering. After those first gluttonous bites ripped away large chunks of flesh, crabs and other small bottom feeders would have long since picked clean the scattered bones of Billy Simms. His remains would now and for always drift with the ebb and flow of the tide along the Middle Passage. Dust to dust.

Billy's widow was lost in thought when Captain Christopher gently took her by the arm. Walking with her a short distance from Peter and Nancy, the Captain reached and brought out a small leather pouch from under his tunic,

"Mrs. Simms, I have here for you and the children the wage for the full voyage which Seaman Simms more than earned. Further, I recommended to the owners of the *Nelly* that the sum of ten pounds sterling be presented in recognition of his faithful service. The *Nelly* never left port, beginning with her maiden voyage, without the services of Billy Simms. And finally, Mrs. Simms, I have added a remembrance of my own for you and yours. The boy who first marched me through the streets of Liverpool at such a young age, barking and directing the locals to make way for the good Captain Christopher, was committed to my well being. It is only fitting that I remember him in this humble fashion. God bless you, Mrs. Simms."

And with that, Captain Christopher returned to his slaver that was now beginning to release her tons of sugar onto the Liverpool docks. Looking over his shoulder, he called to Peter, "And son, don't forget to carry home your father's bag. Good luck to you, boy."

Five years would pass before Nancy Simms would find herself in the right place at the right time. Her long gaze at the docks from the deck of a ship bound for Calais in 1778 would be her last view of Liverpool. Hell, later in the same voyage her over the shoulder glance at the cliffs of Dover would prove to be the last time she would look upon any part of England. Janet would miss her daughter terribly and Nancy would always hold her mother warmly in her heart but Nancy saw the coast of France and beyond as an irresistible adventure not to be missed. She would not be a woman to dwell in the past or wrap herself in false drama. Real people were out and about and moving and doing. Nancy could not be certain of exactly where she would be going but she sensed it was going to be one hell of a ride.

By 1780 Mayer and Gutle Rothschild had grown their family to include their daughter and three sons, Amschel, Salomon and Nathan. Two more sons, Carl and James, would arrive to join their brothers in the coming years. As Mayer and Gutle worked long hours to establish the Rothschild name within the banking circles of Germany and beyond, their sons were trained to trust first and foremost in family while keeping a vigilant eye out for all who schemed to prey upon any successful Jewish business.

"Papa, Papa! They are coming! They are on our street and will be here very soon!" Breathless, Salomon Rothschild had scrambled over the cobblestones of the Judengasse as he raced to give his father this warning.

"Salomon, slow down son and take a breath. Who is coming and why such concern?"

"The men from the city, Papa! The men you showed us. The Frankfurt taxing men have come onto our street, Papa."

Mayer Rothschild put a gentle hand on Salomon's shoulder and assured him, "All will be well, Salomon." Immediately and with conviction, Mayer turned to his wife, "Gutle, help me move everything from the office as we have practiced - quickly now. Amschel, take your brothers and sister to your room and read to them. None of you are to leave the room until I have called for you."

For centuries Frankfurt had functioned as an Imperial Free City, loyal to the Holy Roman Emperor. No local German government or feudal lord controlled the city of Frankfurt. City officials were appointed by Rome and, once installed, these bureaucrats wielded near total control over the daily affairs of the city. Rules that governed commerce for Jews in eighteenth century Frankfurt were extensive and pernicious. First things first, competition from the jew would be eliminated altogether in most trades by simply making it a crime for Jews to participate in almost every business. Within the few permitted areas of legal Jewish commerce, where money changing and banking were included, the local authorities were ruthless in assessing taxes, fees and penalties inside the walls of the Judengasse. At anytime and without notice, officials could demand that all assets of Mayer Rothschild and his licensed bank be reported and presented for their review. Records would be compared to results from their previous inspection. Increases in gold and silver coin deposits, the diamonds, guilders and other valuables held as collateral for loans now recorded on their books, interest that had been earned on monies loaned to their clients – all these sources of value were subject to heavy taxes imposed by Frankfurt officials. Mayer and other members of the Jewish business fraternity had long since pooled their experience and devised practices to try and survive the unjust treatment brought upon their community. While legal objections and petitions for relief would be routinely brought forth, these Jewish business owners knew that little would ever be done on their behalf. No, the men and their wives whose very lives were tied to the survival of their business understood that it was up to them to protect themselves.

With practiced precision Mayer and Gutle moved their designated lock boxes of currency and valuable papers through a concealed series of narrow passages leading to a small vault hidden under a trap door known only to the two of them. Mayer went to great lengths to keep a set of books documenting a modest banking concern. He would then present assets that confirmed that level of activity. The actual scope of this increasingly respected bank was far greater than what Frankfurt officials ever understood. Even so, their tax burden would be heavy. Mayer always worked with the officials to plead for relief and it would always be necessary to grease the palms of those in charge. Eventually an agreement would be reached, bribes funded, taxes paid and all would proceed forward until officials determined that it was time to play the game again.

Mayer Rothschild would not be blessed with the many years that Gutle would enjoy. It was to be from his deathbed in 1812 when his final instructions would be given completing his ingenious design for the financial empire that his sons would so effectively bring forth. The cities where he had painstakingly introduced each son to contacts he had nurtured on their behalf were to be home to the banks that each son would establish. Amschel, as the oldest, was the obvious choice to continue their business in Frankfurt. Salomon would plant the flag in Vienna while Nathan would gain international renown for the direction of the Rothschild franchise in London. Carl would lead the bank in Rome while young James would enjoy tremendous success in Paris. Early in his career Mayer had struggled over a perplexing problem. If you desire to spread your influence across the European horizon, how do you deal with the constant conditions of war and conflict that existed between traditional enemies? Threats to a banking concern trying to move gold across conflicted borders were obvious. In peacetime, threats would come from within as officials that patrolled those same borders would look to take their toll. But the strength of the family bond, the compelling reality of blood being shared in one's veins led Mayer to his answer. The brother in charge of the bank in Paris would simply draw on the bank in London while the leader of the London bank could easily draw on the bank in Rome. Officials and nobility across Europe who might prefer to control the every move of a Jewish banker would lack the reach to come between the sons of Mayer Rothschild. Further, when other houses of finance would be confined by conflict, many of these same officials and nobility would lean on the powerful House of Rothschild to solution their financial needs. Mayer Rothschild addressed his mortality as does every man but his legacy would know no such limit. True genius will not be denied.

Jamie Barnwell was different from any white man I had met. While I had now seen a number of such men I had only met a few. The sailor Billy Simms would prove to be unforgettable and most all of the whites that I had seen I had no desire to meet. They smelled foul, they spoke as if you did not exist, their hands moved over you like you were a dog and if the spirit moved them, you were beat like a hostile thief. No, for a slave such as me the arrival of a white man meant it was time to leave. Nothing good was to come your way when he was present. So as we sailed from St. Croix to the colony of South Carolina I was surprised to be regularly sought out by Mr. Barnwell. My ability to speak the English was very limited and he only spoke a little of the French but he genuinely wanted to talk to me. I had been told by young Hamilton and by my only friend, Nicolas Dumas, that some man at this South Carolina now owned me. At first I just assumed Barnwell was spending time to find out more about me to try and get more money from the man in South Carolina. With each visit we seemed to understand each other better. Always Jamie wanted to know if I had enough to eat and drink. Was the small corner and hammock where I was told to sleep okay? Did I need anything to stay warm at night? Actually, the conditions on the ship were as nice as what I was given on the trip with Dumas and the work I was required to do each day was not too severe. I thanked Barnwell for asking and tried to say as little as possible. Still he had things to tell me. He kept asking questions.

"Prince, the Horry family that bought you, they are good people. The place where you will live is called Chicora Pines. This ship is taking us to Charleston, the most beautiful city in America. The rice fields of Chicora Pines are north, up the coast from Charleston along the Santee River. Did you ever see how the rice fields in Africa were flooded?"

Slowly I shook my head 'no'. I had never worked in flooded fields until I reached Saint-Domingue. Why so many questions? What was this all about?

"Well, I know you worked the sugarcane fields in Saint-Domingue. Flooding the fields and working the crop on Chicora Pines will be similar but I believe you will find the conditions to be easier. South Carolina is hot as hell in the summer but we are so far north of Saint-Domingue. I believe the cooler nights and shorter days will make life a bit more pleasant."

Pleasant? Why in the hell would Mr. Barnwell or any other white man give a damn about how my life in some rice field was going to work out? Before we reached Charleston I must admit that whenever I saw him on ship headed my way I actually hoped that Jamie Barnwell was coming to speak to me. Imagine that! Wanting to speak to a white man. Yes, Jamie Barnwell was different and I was becoming curious about the city they called Charleston.

PRINCE of SAND - Chapter Ten – Quel ami j'ai à Jamie / What a Friend I Have in Jamie

Marie-Jeanne Rose Bertin was thirty-one years old in 1778, a young woman with a long career in front of her. In fact, as an accomplished Parisian designer, Rose could already boast of having the most impressive client list of any salon in either Paris or Versailles. On one of her routine visits to England and bored with the predictable designs presented in London, Rose had accepted an invitation from a successful merchant to visit his estate on the river Mersey. She arrived in Liverpool a few days early. In her carriage, moving along the waterfront, she expressed frustration with her driver who was clearly unfamiliar with the location of her hotel;

"Oh, vous imbécile! Arrêtez le taxi. ... Oh, you imbecile ! Stop the taxi." ... "Certainly there must be someone nearby who can help us find our way." As she scolded the hapless driver, Mademoiselle Bertin stepped away from the carriage and stood, hands on hips, surveying the clamor of the waterfront. Few who understood the intrigues of the French court would have been surprised to learn that Rose Bertin had more on her Liverpool agenda than a social call. The hostilities that seemed to have no end between France and England were about to boil over yet again. Their bloody differences that began in 1778 would be referred to simply as the Anglo-French War. While the British were forced to direct more resources than they had planned across the Atlantic in order to put the colonists in their place, the French raised the ante, particularly at sea. The Spaniards would find it impossible to sit out the unfolding shuffle of imperial interests and would engage themselves in 1779. Understandably there would be a premium on information regarding enemy movements and strategy. Legions of spies and informers would be cultivated as each throne leaned on their generals and admirals for victory at any cost. The stakes were high. Was that not always the case?

It had been six years since a very young Bertin had caught her first big break. Like most new business owners, her first two years after opening her clothing shop, Le

Grand Mogol, had been full of risk and difficulties. It was hard to survive the competition in most any business but for a young girl with so little experience at the hand of Mademoiselle Pagelle to step up and take on the best that Paris had to offer? Le Grand Mogol, indeed. But as those attentive to fashion in Paris and throughout Europe would come to understand, Rose Bertin held an unshakeable belief in one very important part of the equation. Above all else, she believed in Rose Bertin. By 1772 she was adding influential ladies from the nobility of Versailles as her clients when she was introduced to the new Dauphine, Marie Antoinette. Having arrived in France from Austria, Marie Antoinette was also quite young as she began preparations to become the bride of Louis XVI. She loved the style of Rose Bertin and the two became close friends, meeting at least twice each week to plan every detail of the royal trousseau. What had been an interesting new shop where fresh ideas were introduced into Parisian wardrobes, Le Grand Mogol was now becoming something more. In the city that set an international standard for salons hosting the intellectual and creative elite, Le Grand Mogol was now a most fashionable place to be seen and heard.

From the busy waterfront corner and in her native tongue, Rose called out to no one in particular, "Is there not one civilized citizen about who is able to direct a visitor to her hotel?"

To her surprise, the response was direct, to the point and phrased in a young lady's best attempt to speak the French, "Oui, mademoiselle. Comment puis-je être au courant? .. How may I be of service?" And in that brief exchange, Nancy Simms and Rose Bertin became acquainted.

Rose would always remember the exchange fondly. She turned to Nancy, surprised and pleased to hear some French spoken in Liverpool, and commented, "So you speak French. Delightful! It would be most helpful if you were to explain to this dullard driver exactly how to reach my hotel. Would you please be so kind?"

Nancy was holding up her hands and laughing lightly as she spoke up, "Whoa - ralentis s'il te plait – slow down, please. My French is only few words. Slow. I can only do slow."

Now it was Rose who chuckled as she nodded in understanding, "Please, my carriage. Please ride and we can talk."

The right place at the right time – for Nancy Simms this encounter on a busy waterfront corner would send her down the road that defined her adult life. Rose Bertin was not easily impressed. Meeting beautiful women and handsome men dedicated to the finery of Parisian fashion was part of her daily routine. Yet this young lady took her breath away. Nancy Simms turned her head. The young girl who had learned on these very docks that her father would no longer haunt her had grown into one of the most beautiful women in all of Liverpool. The deep auburn in her mother's hair that shone so when the sun was bright had been passed on to Nancy. Billy Simms' sharp and attractive facial features shaped her memorable smile. In Nancy, all of these desirable qualities came together beautifully. Her perfect complexion and shapely bosom on a tall and slender frame brought depth to her attractive appearance. To all of these qualities Nancy brought that which she and Mademoiselle Bertin shared so well. From parents who knew next to nothing about engaging with others in a meaningful way came a self assured young lady as inquisitive as she was confident. Rose would feel as though she was looking in a mirror while Nancy would become both friend and beneficiary to Bertin's largesse. The carriage ride to the hotel led to an evening together over as fine a dinner as Nancy had yet seen. Nancy's language skills, first realized as she parroted the conversations of sailors from around the world who brought their business to the tavern where Janet worked, helped convince her to jump at the chance to accompany Rose back to France. Their initial discussion had to do with the idea that Nancy would simply go back with Bertin for a long visit. She and Rose explained to Janet that, after a two month visit in Paris, Nancy would return to Liverpool with the benefit of having some initial training as a dress maker under her belt. The fact that hostilities between France and England would prevent her return would overshadow the fact that Nancy would have never left Paris to return to the city of her childhood. Once in Paris, once embraced as a member of the creative force that was the staff of Le Grand Mogol, Nancy would be taking flight. If you are hard at work in the taverns of Liverpool one day only to find yourself a few weeks later observing the style and grace of those in Versailles who see to the needs of the Queen of France, you will not be ready to leave. Nancy joined Bertin in Paris in 1778. Ten years would pass before she would even consider leaving Paris on some other adventure.

The courtier from King Louis' Foreign Office had been rather blunt in his approach to recruit Rose Bertin. As the mademoiselle had now long been a frequent visitor in Versailles and with her contacts in Paris growing daily, the reach from the royal officer was straightforward. "Miss Bertin, your service to the Queen is well recognized and no doubt highly valued by both Her Highness and His Majesty, the King. Clearly, your professional diligence has made you welcome within circles of influence on the continent where you are well regarded. With respect, the throne suggests that you are strategically positioned to help your country. Information gathered, Miss Bertin, and understanding how certain information is shared within circles of influence can be quite valuable to the royal family. Your King asks that you give consideration to furthering the cause of France. You will be trained in the art of securing valuable information. There will be guidance as to where and when your targets are to be pursued. The crown will compensate you handsomely for information that is shared in a timely fashion for you see, Miss Bertin, and it is important that you understand, that the risks taken by those who handle such circumstances well can be overwhelming. Do you understand what is being asked of you, mademoiselle?"

Rose sat silently holding eye contact with this diplomat as she took her time before responding. After some minutes had passed, she spoke in a calm and clear voice, " Monsieur, the foreign office flatters me to suggest that a dress maker from the streets of Paris could make a meaningful contribution in the work you describe. The King can rest assured that I will do what I can for France. Having said that, please advise your superiors that my heart belongs to our Queen. Her Majesty has made clear my path to success. If there is some way for me to possibly help the Queen, this is something I must be involved in. Let the risk be damned."

Smiling, the gentleman rose from his chair bowing slightly to Rose. "Somehow I expected a patriotic response. This conversation will now be relayed to my superiors in Versailles. Miss Bertin, you will find that change comes quickly in our world of espionage as old news has no value. Moving quickly, but always with discretion, is our constant challenge."

"Yes, I understand. What is the next step? How do we proceed?" was Rose's response.

Moving to the door, the agent shrugged slightly and said, "Within a few days you will be contacted by your control agent. This individual will serve as your director. For your safety, this is someone unknown to me. In the meantime, listen carefully and observe closely. It seems the smallest things tend to make the greatest difference. Take care of yourself, Mademoiselle Bertin."

Charleston was unlike any town I had ever seen. Our ship ran down the length of Sullivan's Island before rounding the point and entering the harbor. As we neared the docks I could clearly see the fortifications, the battery, that gave definition to the

town named for King Charles. The array of fine homes lining the battery on streets that led into town was impressive. In Charleston, one got the feeling that the people who settled the colony of South Carolina were proud as hell of their busy port and all who came here under sail would be dazzled by her grandeur before an anchor could even be dropped.

Jamie Barnwell was comfortable in most any setting but he was absolutely in his element when out and about in his hometown of Charleston. From the moment he could be seen on deck as they neared their mooring the calls began to drift across the water, "Well look what the sea has turned up today! Mr. James T. Barnwell, himself!" … "Jamie T. Barnwell is back in town! Lock up your whiskey and hide all the women!" … "Old Charles Town will dance a jig tonight – James Thomas Barnwell is back with new tales to tell!" Jamie shook his head, shared in the laughter and waived happily to his friends. Charleston, one of the oldest and largest towns in all the colonies, opened her arms to embrace one of her own. It had been a profitable trip for the firm of Begbie and Barnwell. Jamie had executed trades skillfully in bringing a ship full of sugar and coffee safely back to South Carolina. With the assistance of young Alexander Hamilton working for Beekman and C ruger in Saint Croix, Barnwell had set in motion a series of orders to be filled and trades to be made that would prove to be clever indeed. But it was his timely negotiation for and purchase of the slave from Saint-Domingue on behalf of the Horry family at Chicora Pines that would make the journey truly memorable. It was late in the afternoon in the office of his company located just a few doors up from St. Phillips Church on Church Street that Jamie introduced his client, Mr. Richard Horry, to Prince;
"Mr. Horry, allow me to present for your inspection and approval this quality slave discovered in Christiansted while outward bound from Port Au Prince. His experience flooding the sugarcane fields of Saint-Domingue while helping direct the African crews on the largest plantation along the Artibonite River will, I feel certain, make him a valuable part of Chicora Pines."

Mr. Richard Middleton Horry stood and faced me, his eyes measuring my demeanor in an unblinking stare as he circled around his new property,
"Do you like to run?" he asked. "Are you one of those god damned runners?"
"No monsieur", was my response. "I stay home."
"God damn good answer", responded my new "master". "I've sent men and hounds as far as the shipyards and rum stills of Rhode Island to drag my niggers back to Chicora Pines. Ask these boys on my plantation. They'll tell you the same." He stood directly in

front of me moving into my space. His nose was almost touching my chin. After a long silence he stepped away saying, "I believe we have an understanding, Mr. Prince. We are cutting new canals in the rice fields and hundreds here from Africa need to be watched closely. Do your job well and you will be well fed."

With that said, he turned to his foreman and gave an order, "Ben, when we reach Chicora Pines get this Prince set up in cabin six and tell the other black niggers in that shed to treat him right. Have Prince give direction to the crew on the new southwest canal and we will find out before supper if he knows what the hell he is doing. Tell him to talk African talk to as many as he can and get them working the right way. If that all goes well, we will know – we will know if we got one fine nigger or not." He then turned to Jamie. "Mr. Barnwell, I don't know just how you do it but you do seem to have a damn fine eye for spottin' a good nigger. I've gotta' tell you, Jamie. If I saw a nigger with a crippled hand walking around the docks of Christiansted, I wouldn't have given him a second look. But here he is, a French speaking canal man! Who the hell would have thought of that? Signed, sealed, delivered pretty-as-you-please, the smartest new nigger to ride up the lane to Chicora Pines in a long damn time. You are a good trader, Jamie Barnwell, and I'm grateful that you represent Chicora Pines."

Now I had turned my shoulders so I was directly facing Jamie, my face turned away from owner Horry. I held my stare as Barnwell was looking down at his shoes. Quickly he glanced up and our eyes met. Just as quickly he cut his eyes back to the floor. "Well, Mr. Horry, you take care and, as always, let me know when I can be of assistance. I will not set sail on my next trading voyage without being certain that I know exactly what the needs are for Chicora Pines before I leave. Good day to you, Richard, and please give Felicia my best."

For a few days I wondered if I would ever see Jamie Barnwell again but I did not think on it for long. The white man comes into your life, you are chained to heavy burdens and pain and the white man passes on leaving you to your long days of sweat and hard work - always, the hard work. Work that can never be completed as each season brought forward a fresh list of demanding tasks that would be repeated without end. For as long as the fall followed the summer, for as long as the winter gave way to spring the work of a slave would continue. The grave was your end, your relief from the orders and the constant demands. Swing low, sweet chariot.

The slaves at Chicora Pines were both the same as all slaves and yet they were different. The slave in the 'cane of Saint-Domingue sang the same sad song as the nigger at Chicora Pines. Now, however, at Chicora Pines I met both slaves from Africa and also more and more slaves born here in the Low Country of South Carolina. The low country niggers were more comfortable living in this marsh area by the sea. It was all they had ever known. While they begged me to tell them of hunts on the plains of Dahomey stalking the king, the lion, they could only imagine such a scene. Often they would call to me, "Prince, please tell us one of your stories" but just as often I was asking them to tell me more about the marsh. Late into the night I listened as they explained the marsh. The movement of the tide drove your schedule for the day. They spoke about crabs, an odd creature that works the bottom of the sandy and muddy creeks, about different fish, the possum and the fox, deer, ducks and geese, the beautiful white herron and more birds of every description. The local slave at Chicora Pines had names for all of this wildlife and I was schooled in their importance to my well being. No white man, not even Richard Middleton Horry, could keep a nigger from catching a fish or cracking a crab! In only a matter of days I was amazed to learn just how expert some of the men in cabin six were at setting their nets to gather an odd fish. This fish had two eyes on the same side of his head and one white side with no eye that always faced the floor of the marsh. This flounder was ugly to see but wonderful to eat. These men had wire traps that sat on the muddy bottom of the marsh. They drove a painted stake into the marsh and tied their trap to the stake. The color of the stake told others who owned that trap. Taking another man's trap was a crime that the niggers would deal with quickly within their own system. Inside the cage would be some kind of bait – the neck of a chicken or a fresh piece of fish called mullet. The tide would flood the marsh covering all the traps. After the water began to recede with the next tide, the owners inspected their traps. It was amazing to see just how many of the striking blue and white crabs, with slight markings of orange, could fit themselves into one cage trying to pinch off a piece of mullet or chicken! I was interested to learn more about fishing but it was running a line of crab traps that captured my imagination.

Yes, the marsh life was different and the possibility for controlling at least a small part of your own life was captivating for me. At times, it was also cold. As you know, I was raised on the heated plains of Africa. All my days spent in Saint-Domingue had one thing in common – they were hot as hell. The fall and spring in the low country are mostly quite pleasant but there are days in winter when the blow comes out of the northeast. Fortunately for me, the foreman at Chicora Pines who ruled over cabin six made sure that new niggers in his area had something warm to wear, including shoes, for the winter months. It made sense. If your plan is to push a man hard for six days out of every week, you know he needs to be warm in winter or he will not work for shit. With a rough shirt made of wool, a pair of leather shoes and an old blanket on my bunk I would make it through my first low country winter. Still, my body told me I was growing older. My hand was not as reliable in winter. Like the crab, my left hand would always be workable as a claw. The two fingers pinched neatly against the thumb allowing me to handle most any task. But in December at Chicora Pines the hand was slow to move each morning. The cold reached into the bone and my left hand simply refused to work as it did in July. One finger, what had been my middle finger, was bent in a way that it would never straighten out anyway.

It was early in March of 1773 on a sparkling fresh spring morning. I can close my eyes and tell what I saw when Jamie Barnwell was riding up the long drive that delivered guests to the Horry mansion. I must tell you, I lost my breath. My disappointment in watching him turn and leave me to my new masters at Chicora Pines so many months ago instantly gave way to an overwhelming hope that I would have a chance to visit with Jamie. Whenever I saw this man, I felt as if I was watching a friend approach. Yes, I will say it, it did not make much sense, but it felt that way all the same. It was not my place to pay any attention to the comings and goings of white folk at the big house and this morning was no exception. It was an easy decision to simply go on about my chores. I will tell you though, I was highly aware of who was walking up to the Horry front door. Chores around the house were seldom difficult. I was never a house nigger, living inside the walls of the magnificent home that sparkled in its grandeur, but as someone who helped direct the field niggers, my duties, when not knee deep in the mud of the canals, were somewhat easier than others in cabin six. You can only imagine my focus on the doors to the master's house once I knew that Mr. Barnwell was inside. Trying not to become too anxious, I finished gathering the fallen limbs and yard trash that needed attention. My job finished, it was time for me to walk back to my cabin and enjoy a few precious hours of time to myself.

As I strolled across the lawn and began to move down the sandy wagon trail that led west from the big house toward the slave cabins, I heard the voice of Ben, the foreman who had command over all us niggers at Chicora Pines. "Prince, whoa Prince! Come here to the back door. Master Horry wants to speak to you."

Of course, I did as I was told, but I knew. As soon as he called my name, I knew. Just as I know there is legend that the Man in the Moon is named ol' Joey McMahon, I knew it was Jamie B. who wanted to speak with me. Old man Horry did not know me from any other nigger on his lawn. Mr. Barnwell was visiting from Charleston and I was instructed to come to the back door. I felt sure that I would have some time to talk to Barnwell but I had no idea about what happened next. Ben led me into the hallway on the back of the house and showed me into a small room with a table and a few chairs. Right behind us came Jamie, "Prince, oh it is good to see you! Prince, you look well. Please, how have you been?"

Honestly, I was surprised but not really. I have shared with you that this man, this James Thomas Barnwell of Charleston, treated me as his friend. But you will also understand that niggers on Chicora Pines were not accustomed to having white friends come a-callin'! Any disappointment or angst I had carried with me from Jamie's last leaving was out the window. I smiled as we shook hands. I believe he reached out to squeeze my right shoulder. "Mr. Barnwell, I am good with thank you. You too are good look. Did you ride today from the Charles Town?"

Jamie ignored my mistakes with the English as he nodded his head, "Yes, my friend. I left Charleston yesterday and stayed with my friends, the Rhetts, in Georgetown last night. I hope you will approve my message and be prepared to travel this afternoon."

Puzzled, I responded, "Message?"

"Prince, please, we will sit." Now alone at the small table, he explained, "I wrote to Mr. Horry a few weeks ago. My work in Charleston and in the islands has kept me very busy. I am now home to stay for at least two months and I have many personal projects around my home that I need to complete. Many tasks will require more than one man and I need someone to work beside me. I asked Mr. Horry if I might be able to hire your services for a period of six weeks. He has agreed to my request but, of course, I would only suggest that we travel back to Charleston together if such an arrangement meets with your approval. Is this something you can agree with?"

Stunned. My mouth must have hung open and if no tear squeezed away from the corner of my eye it was only because I was so surprised. My mind raced as I slowly nodded my head in agreement. All of my instincts were correct. I was sitting at the table with a friend – a friend who I would never doubt again. But again my mind screamed, "Why!"

I have had friends at Chicora Pines. Nicolas Dumas, the Creole from Port-Au-Prince, he was a special friend who had made it possible for me to avoid death in the fields of 'cane. The friends of my youth, Mamout, Malek and Batou, I have told you of these good friends. Often when I was asleep I dreamed about hunting with Mamout and Batou. When we are awake we are required to deal with the reality that is in front of us. When we dream, our true self is free to come forward. When you are a prisoner and you have been taken far from your home, you still continue to carry your home in your dreams. So I had many friends and now Jamie sat before me. When I finally die, I will still look at this man with some wonder in my eyes.

"Excellent!" was Jamie's comment. "I just knew you would be ready for a change. Please, Prince," he said as he handed me a burlap bag, "please gather your things as we will want to leave for Charleston right away. I have brought an extra horse and saddle with me and they are being watered and fed as we speak."

We both knew that it would take no time for me to gather my pitiful 'things'. I hurried to cabin six and placed my extra shirt in the bag, returning to the yard just as quickly. My mind was frightened, "Oh Vordun, what if he has already gone? What if there is some mistake and Mr. Horry says I cannot go?" But my fears were misplaced. Jamie was already in the saddle and an attendant, a young white man, actually held the reins as I scrambled up onto my horse. And with that, I was riding down the lane, side-by-side with my friend, riding at our leisure to the Charles Town many miles to the south! "Vordun, you are smiling on Prince this day. Tomorrow I will get a healthy chicken and fill your bowl with his blood. Oh thank you, Vordun, and please do not leave me."

PRINCE of SAND - Chapter Eleven – Les Folies de Barnwell et Morrison / The Antics of Barnwell and Morrison

Charleston in the colony of South Carolina in 1773 was like a dream to me except my dreams were on the Dahomey plain and this was next to the Atlantic Ocean in a place owned and run by white men. I cannot tell you how it felt to stay in the Barnwell home and be treated as a human being. Day after day I would lift my head from the pillow on my bed. Quickly my mind would clear as I recognized where I was while a sigh of relief escaped over my smiling lips. Every time, I would relax, returning my head to that pillow of feathers. I would stretch my toes down to the far end of the bed, rolling to the coolest part of the cotton sheets. I do not know what it is to lie down upon a cloud but I cannot imagine that it brings more pleasure. Most mornings Jamie would have already been up and walked the ten blocks or so from his house on Water Street to the office of Begbie and Barnwell. I was teaching him the French. He was teaching me the English. He would try to write out a list of chores for me to work on using the French. My job was to try and complete the tasks and write down my work on the paper using the English. Yes, I was happier when I was at home on the Dahomey Plain. Of course I was! I was a free man in my home and held my head high with the respect of all in our village. But these days in Charleston reminded me that life could be worth living. With a handshake and a smile Jamie reminded me that I have friends. My name in our family was Yamar but in the village I was simply known as Prince and yes, I have many friends. The days were pleasant and seemed to fly by but in the evenings, when Jamie returned, the cooler part of day brought with it long hours of an ongoing discussion between good friends. It was, quite simply, hopeful.

Many homes in Charleston are sideways to the street. Storage space and tack rooms go on the ground floor where frequent flooding might ruin the fine furnishings that would never grace these spaces. Long porches reach across the side of the homes on the second floor designed to benefit from fair breezes. Beautiful rooms for dining, sitting rooms and often the master bedroom dazzle one on this second level and a well appointed kitchen for final preparation and serving of food would be found near the back of the rooms, farthest from the street. Additional bedrooms and a library could often be found on the third level. My room was all the way in the back, tucked in next to the kitchen, on the second level. Often the top house nigger or favored maid would take such a room. You would walk the length of the home on the second floor porch to reach my door which was a separate entrance leading only into this single room. To me, it was perfect in every way. Jamie laughed and told me it was now known as the Perch of the Prince. I waved my finger back and forth and, in a serious tone, advised him that should he fail to show proper respect to his Royal visitor, he might well find himself sleeping on the High Battery at low tide. And we would laugh. Oh Vordun, after all the tears, after carrying the stench of the second deck during the Middle Passage with me for over twenty years, having watched men and families being shattered as they were moved through the slave auctions and after endless years in the shit sugarcane of Saint Domingue which just ate men up in short periods of time – after all of this I was sitting with a friend talking and laughing long into the night.

The laughter was what separated Jamie Barnwell from any other man I ever knew. He just had a way, a genius about him when it came to finding humor that the rest of us never seemed to notice. I will give you an example. Walking down Church Street at the busy corner with Trade Street we saw a slave walking toward us, clearly heading back to his owner's big house following a day of work on another structure. The man and his clothes were speckled, covered with tiny drops of a soft cream color that was all over him. With no more than a quick glance shared between them, Jamie nodded slightly to the stranger and asked, "Paintin'?" Without hesitation or slowing his gait, the response came, "No, plasterin". Both men chuckled slightly as they passed on in different directions. In such common circumstances, Jamie found a common thread with almost anyone. When the white men and their ladies walked along the colorful streets of Charleston, slave niggers moved themselves off of the walkway and into the street. Huge slave men kept their eyes looking down to their feet as smaller men in their fine clothes sauntered past, taking particular care not to gaze upon the ladies that might be among them. These little men, strutting like the smallest rooster in the yard, never saw the slaves that cleared their path. Their eyes could not see. But it was different when James Barnwell of Begbie and Barnwell took to walking about town. Black men who cleared Jamie's path received a tip of his cap or a slight nod as this Barnwell tried to look them in the eye. Many slaves might recognize him and mumble their, "Mornin', Mistah Barnwell" as we passed, always receiving some common courtesy of recognition in response. And then, from time to time, there would be the black man who Jamie had come to know well and they would inevitably trade local stories and gossip when they crossed each other's paths. Barnwell was simply different from most any white man in this way. White or black, young or old, Jamie had friends spread throughout Charleston and the surrounding Low Country. He possessed the uncanny ability to mix as comfortably with Senator Cotesworth Pinkney as he did with Peanut Johnson, one of the black slaves who frequented the corners of Meeting Street dancing for pennies and cigars. Truth be told, both men were friends of Barnwell. And the truth is Jamie probably preferred the company of Peanut to most any other friend he had.

Peanut Johnson and Jamie shared some long nights with jugs of rum which led them into some spots out on the edge of town and out into the low country where few white men were ever welcome. The stories that unfolded were epic but rarely told by Jamie. He simply left it to others to recount the frivolity and adventure while he simply went about the business of being himself. Peanut and Jamie understood one another on a level known only by true friends. Early on in their friendship Peanut was in line to sign up for a local work detail down by the lower battery. His plan was to work a full day and earn seventy-five cents to put toward a pair of shoes and perhaps a spot of rum. The foreman organizing the group asked each nigger to call out his name.

"Fred Johnson!" rang forth from Peanut when asked. Later in the month, Peanut's neighbor on his street was making a list for their local church. He asked, "Peanut, what be your real name fo' de minister at de church?"

"Andy Johnson!" came Peanut's proud response.

With his hand on his chin and after studying on this response for a few minutes, Jamie looked at Peanut and asked, "Peanut, I know you were 'Fred Johnson' working on the battery a few weeks ago. Now, this morning, you tell your church group that you be 'Andy Johnson'. Who the hell are you, Peanut?"

Without hesitation and with a gleam in his eye, Peanut turned to Jamie and reported, "Jamie, Fred Johnson be my work name and Andy Johnson be my church name." After a brief pause and with a grin growing across his face, he looked at Jamie and as he shrugged he announced, "Peanut be my *party* name!"

This particular Saturday morning was cool and a bit breezy as Jamie and I moved along East Bay Street toward the market to gather provisions to be carried back to Water Street. Then I looked up into the nightmare. Looking straight ahead, the water and the docks were three blocks off to my right. I saw them, the line of slaves being marched across Trade Street as they were herded toward the low slung open air brick structure two blocks to my left. Glancing quickly to my right, I knew what my eye would find. There, floating at the dock, the three masts of the ship that had just unloaded these tortured souls. Son of a bitch! The men were secured to each other at the ankle and some also at the neck. So familiar! Children tried to stay in actual touch of their mothers, orphans to a woman they might recognize. All seemed confused and every one of them seemed to glisten in the sunlight. Each had rubbed the other with oil from buckets on the deck as ordered last night or this morning. My knees were like jelly and I thought I would crumble into the street. Then I saw him! Shit! Vordun, why? Why do you torture me so! The young man, surely sixteen years of age, stumbling forward, his eyes as large as saucers and he seemed to look right at me – only me! Yes, I was looking into a mirror that was twenty years old. It may as well have been me, that youngster who moved in such obvious fear, and his stare would haunt me for many years.

Jamie watched me watching them and immediately understood. Taking my elbow to offer support, he asked if I was feeling ok. I simply looked at him and said, "I think it is the good time for me at Water Street." Jamie nodded and I was off on my way.

Taking a direct route, you can walk from the Barnwell house on Water Street to the market on East Bay within twenty minutes. On this day I wandered through Charleston for almost two hours before reaching the house. Once inside the gate, I found a patch of shade next to a large magnolia at the back of the side yard. Sitting with my back to the street facing the tree I tried to keep my mind from that line of slaves but they crowded me in an uncomfortable way. It did not seem fair that I enter the comfort of the house while they stood on blocks to be inspected and fondled by the men with money, so I remained in the yard. It was suppertime when Jamie returned home and called me inside.

Our discussion that night was only about one subject - one man owning another. "How can it continue to happen?", I asked. Jamie shrugged and spoke of the huge farms and plantations. "Prince, you have said that the sugarcane fields in Saint-Domingue were large?"

"Yes, they seemed to never end", was my reply.

"We both know that the Horry land for rice at Chicora Pines is huge."

"Truly, I have never seen the end of Chicora Pine."

"Prince, man is evil in the treatment of his brother. The strong have hunted the weak for as long as the wind has blown. You have told me that your tribe was not weak but you and your friends were hunting far from the village?" he asked,

"Yes. We were men on the great hunt and we were children playing in the forest", came the answer I had explained to myself endlessly over the past twenty years.

We sat silent for a long period. Jamie sipped rum from a cup and I poured some as well. This was not my normal practice.

"It is a terrible price you are forced to pay for the silly mistake of youth", said Jamie in an effort to make me feel better.

"And why, Jamie? Why must so many continue to pay such a price?" I could hear a bitter edge in my voice as I stared at my friend.

"One word, my unlucky friend. The word is "greed" or "avidité" in the French. You can only imagine that strong tribes around this world would someday say, "I have enough" and yet that message is never delivered. You told me you reached Saint-Domingue on a ship called the *Nelly*. Can you recall who sold you to the *Nelly* captain?" Barnwell asked.

I looked at him and nodded, "The grand nigger Jaja, the man called 'King of the Trade' in that part of Africa. It seemed he owned everything."

"And he is strong?" asked Jamie.

"Very."

After many minutes and just before we finally went to our beds I looked at Jamie Barnwell and said, "You are my friend. Please, I ask you, please buy me from Chicora and I will work for as long as you say. Please?"

Something changed in that moment as Jamie turned away slightly. Just as quickly he turned back, "I cannot. Prince, please try to understand. I have faced this situation often and will continue to do so as for as long as I live. I simply cannot purchase the burdens of every troubled friend, even as good a friend as you and even in the face of the crime of slavery. Please, I ask that you not judge but try to understand. I can see, however, that such an answer must ring empty and you may no longer want me for your friend."

I was truly alone when that net dropped upon me so long ago. Tonight I recognized once again that the Prince was walking through this life on my own. It seems to me that I actually smiled weakly at Barnwell and said, "No, old Jamie. I do not want to lose you as a friend. My path is lonely enough as it is. I will complete every chore you can find as I wish to remain on Water Street as long as you can keep me." I could understand what Jamie was saying. And I must say that I was deeply disappointed in my friend.

Jamie almost jumped up from the table, glad, I feel sure, to have this conversation end. "Excellent my friend. I have something special in store for tomorrow evening and will be working on my friend, Charlton Morrison, to help me with the arrangements. Your job for tomorrow, Sir Prince, will be to share in our fun!"

Jamie could make me laugh. It was not lost on me that years had passed in my life when I failed to even share a smile with anyone else. Jamie seemed to make something special out of ordinary situations. Walking up from the Battery the next evening on Church Street, Jamie began to laugh out loud. Before I could ask the reason, Jamie was pulling me into a trot as we ran two blocks to the home of his friend, Charlton Morrison. Over cups of rum Jamie cajoled and harassed Charlton to bring out one of his pistols and join him in his prank. I waited outside enjoying a sip of rum on the porch. Jamie and Charlton emerged as Jamie explained that the newlywed couple living up the street, Cheshire and Francis Palmer Owen, were regularly closing their shades and retiring earlier and earlier in the evening having recently returned home from a grand wedding trip to Virginia. It made perfect sense to Jamie that a pistol, loaded with powder but no ball so as to assure injury would be avoided, needed to be fired outside of the bride's bedroom as an excited reaction was sure to follow. Against his better judgment and somewhat swayed by dark rum, Charlton prepared the pistol and the two quickly arrived at the Owen home further up Water Street. They directed me to sit in a far corner of the yard. My role was to try and absorb the big picture around the house watching all that would unfold when the big moment arrived. They chuckled to themselves as the two Charleston natives talked their way past Robert, the doorman, while squawking about it being of utmost importance that they bring critical news to Mr. Owen right away.

Now this was not as easy a task as it may seem. You see Robert, doorman for the Owen household, had been a house nigger for the family since the age of six when his mother had served as cook for old Mr. & Mrs. Owen. Hell, he had helped raise Cheshire. Robert Owen was as distinguished a black man as you would hope to find in all of the Low Country and damn proud of it. No, it took some mighty fast talking for Barnwell and Morrison to breeze by ol' Robert.

Once past this barrier, twenty seconds had not passed before the shot rang out with Barnwell and Morrison standing on either side of the bedroom door.

For years to come, Jamie would shed tears as he laughed at his own eyewitness description of the chaos that unfolded. Apparently the amorous couple had been on top of the bed covers fully entangled with one another without their night clothes which had been set aside. Francis Palmer Owen had jumped halfway to the door before running straight into the middle of the drawing room, naked as she could be. Cheshire Owen had come charging out just behind his bride only to crash headlong into Robert. Unsettled by Mr. Owen's friends having charged past him through the front door, Robert had come racing across the sitting room from the foyer with nothing but the worst possible fears screaming through his head after the pistol erupted. All five paused in the middle of the room for a long silent moment before Mrs. Owen screamed, Mr. Owen cursed and Robert fainted on the couch. I was curled up in a ball under a bush as I watched the two invaders sprint down the porch, cross the street and run laughing into the night. Silently I slipped across the street and caught up with Jamie at his home within the hour. I sat and listened as Jamie and Charlton congratulated each other on a trick whose success had surpassed their wildest dream. Then they urged me to describe the scene from my perch in the yard. They doubled over at my description of the riotous event. The delicious details were shared in such a manner as to respect the bride's decency while taking their good friend Cheshire to task. The fact that I had been invited to play an "innocent bystander" role would never be mentioned to anyone else. This would spare me my neck and the Owen's unnecessary embarrassment. Good fun was good fun and Jamie Barnwell produced more than his fair share. I understood the act to be frivolous and immature. It was also light and funny. Men of all races from four different continents had been regularly going to extreme measures to flood my life with darkness and pain. Thank god for at least one moment of light and funny. I thanked Vordun for Jamie Barnwell.

PRINCE of SAND – Chapter Twelve – Notre monde, il se développe plus petit / Our World, It Grows Smaller

The sharing of secrets in Paris and Versailles took more out of Rose Bertin than she had expected. Truly, it seemed as if every other person she was in contact with was an agent for some country or trading house full of information wrapped in intrigue. Her advisors had warned she might be overwhelmed early. They suggested she treat information received with healthy skepticism. Still, it was difficult not to be taken in. Part of her seemed to want all of the whispered secrets to be true and meaningful. Her mind was always turning over the different threads, trying to weave together a map as to where all this information led. This practice of thinking ahead, this scheming mind that Rose indulged is like many habits. Taken in moderation, the results can be healthy and invigorating. Over indulge and you are at risk. You risk losing your perspective as reality is blurred. Such behavior is unhealthy for any citizen. For someone in Rose's new world the risks were enlarged. Perhaps her sense for the dramatic would work against her. She needed to draw on a steady personality that would not easily be confused or swayed by gossip or false news.

It was 1783, seven years following the excitement in the colonies of America when the leaders of that revolution had declared their independence. Now, in Paris, with seven years of stifling the British efforts to bring them to their knees behind them, the representatives of what they now called a United States of America were the victor. Officials from both the U.S.A. and Great Britain were in The City of Lights to sign what would be known as the Treaty of Paris. It was official. The peace had been won. The revolution was over. Or was it ?

France in 1783 was a hotbed of new ideas and political debate. The French played an integral part in supporting the American experiment. American men and women had struggled to crawl out from under British rule and France was only too pleased to help reduce British influence in the New World. The great general and diplomat who had such a positive impact on key American leaders, General Lafayette, now championed the cause of freedom within French citizenry. By 1785 the seeds of the French Revolution would begin to take hold. Little did they know, but the royal houses of

Europe would soon enough feel their world shifting beneath their feet. Nothing would be quite the same after Lord Cornwallis had surrendered to General George Washington at Yorktown in the colony, now the state, of Virginia.

Lafayette could not and would not leave his passion for the rights of freemen to speak and share ideas openly behind in Virginia when he returned to France. By 1787 his close friend, former Virginia governor Thomas Jefferson, would join him in Paris serving as America's Minister to France. Between them they drew on Jefferson's work from his new nation's Bill of Rights as Lafayette came forward introducing to France the "Declaration of the Rights of Man and of the Citizen", a statement that brought forth deafening silence from Versailles. Of course, most any of the well read in either America, England or France would be quick to note that the true original work from whence these remarkable revolutionary dissertations grew was that of Squire George Mason, the distinguished author of the "Virginia Declaration of Rights" which he had made public in 1776. Mason, a successful plantation owner in Virginia on property over looking the Potomac River, lived only a few miles south of Mount Vernon and his friend, General Washington. Mount Vernon and Mason's Gunston Hall housed two giants who played leading roles in reshaping the human condition during those remarkable years.

What did this mean for Rose Bertin and her ongoing work to clothe the Queen, Marie Antoinette? As she developed state secrets to benefit the throne, could she continue to direct her now flourishing shop, La Grand Mogul? It meant that she was very busy. So busy that she desperately needed more than a helper. She needed a confidant, a companion. Someone who could help her think through the intrigues, to help execute strategies that required careful coordination. Of course, this meant exposing another individual to the risks associated with living as a spy. Such stress is not for everyone but Rose knew where she would always find a willing and capable partner. Nancy Simms nearly squealed with glee when Rose first approached regarding clandestine activities. While she never pretended to match Rose when it came to the world of fine fashion, Nancy more than held her own matching one agent against another. It seemed the more uncertain the circumstances, the more determined and focused agent Simms became. And if the truth were known, Nancy was less committed to the causes of France than she was to the adrenaline that surged when danger was in the air.

The older gentleman from Spain had been visiting the Mogul frequently these past few weeks. His taste for fine women's wear and wine varied with each visit while his attention to Nancy never wavered. Working from a rear fitting area within the shop, Nancy moved easily from busy salons on the first and third floors. Only occaisionally would she entertain a local walk-in client on the second floor where original Bertin designs were modeled and displayed. The Spaniard followed her now up the narrow staircase that was used almost exclusively by staff. Nancy quickened her pace after continuing past the second floor moving up to the third level where she stepped into the hallway leading down the left side of the building. She paused on the last stair, breathing harder as she listened for the steps of her determined pursuer. As he gained the top step and moved onto the rich oriental carpet running the length of the hallway, Senor Carlos Montague was surprised to have his right hand covered by her cool smooth fingers. Nancy took him by the hand. He thought she had winked her eye as he followed her down the hall to the third door on the left. Her fresh and subtle fragrance led him into the room tastefully appointed with fine antique chairs and small tables for cards or backgammon. Some of the art and mirrors hanging on the walls were gifts to Rose from the Daulphin. Turning to face him and now taking both his hands in hers, Nancy curtsied ever so slightly and spoke,

"Good afternoon, Senor. I am Mademoiselle Nancy Simms, here to entertain the Senor and I do so hope you have time to share a brandy?"

Enjoying the flattery, Senor Montague bowed from the waist, his eyes never moving from hers. In the French, he graciously accepted the brandy as the two exchanged pleasantries. The Senor would have been well advised to limit the brandy to a single sniffer and, in hindsight, he most certainly would have made certain to have one of his Spaniard companions along side. The aging Senor Montague had been working as an assistant Charge de Affairs in Spain's foreign office to France for over fifteen years. While certain senior diplomats preferred to roam the halls of Versailles as they committed themselves to unraveling the secrets within King Louis's court, Carlos Montague had long since become rather bored with palace drama. No, the Senor much preferred the gay excitement to be found in the City of Lights. Let others anxious to promote their young careers lock themselves within the gates of the palace. The wise and colorful Montague would spend his time helping manage official business in the Paris office by day while drinking deeply of the seemingly endless delights that Parisians enjoyed after dark.

In our village on the Dahomey plain it is the lion who holds the place of honor when we give thanks for the animals that we hunt. We do so to bring strength to our children. We praise Vordun and we honor the lion. You learn that the lion leading the pride will often take part in the kill. He will move when it is time to bring down the prey that will deliver strength both to him and to his cubs. But first this male will wait. It is the women in his pride who will stalk and give chase. The prey will be caught by surprise. The hunted that are fleet will take flight and gain confidence as they move quickly across their path of escape. Sadly for the hunted, they will quickly learn that the first female has simply flushed them and moved this victim toward her waiting sisters. Now it will not take long for the story to end. Most often, the leader of the pride is the first to taste blood from the kill.

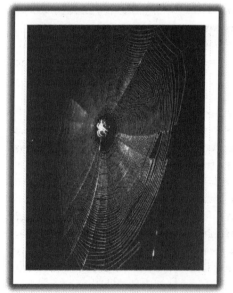

Vordun is proud of the lion while Ruthella, our spirit of calm and serenity, teaches us to study the ways of the spider. Look at the open space chosen by the spider for her web. It is large and exposed to the wind yet she goes ahead with her task. From a perch well above her chosen space she begins. The first strand is attached. She then lowers herself from her device down to the bottom of the trap. With this first strand in place, she goes about her business. Focused, determined and hungry, she takes her time to get it right, one strand at a time. Once in place, her web is poised to bear fruit. Now, just as the leader of the pride, the spider will rest and wait. Her target will struggle, without success, when she scurries across the web to finish the kill.

Nancy Simms and Rose Bertin were never called on to finish the kill. There would always be large men a plenty with feathers on their hats and medals on their chests ready and waiting for opportunities to send in other men to sink the knife. No, Rose and Nancy spent their time flushing prey. They helped move soldiers and ships toward traps. And make no mistake, they learned to be very effective in their chosen occupation.

The brandy was superb and quickly consumed. Skillfully, agent Simms put Senor Montague at ease and treated him to the kind of seductive interlude that most any man finds intoxicating. The door in the far corner of the sitting room next to the window opened into a smaller room where a day bed, covered with a feather comforter, was waiting. Late in the afternoon, the satisfied Senor rose from the bed and began to collect his scattered clothes. He shook his head slightly turning a wry smile to Nancy as he spoke,

"You young ladies of Paris never cease to amaze. My dear Nancy, an afternoon with you alone is a dream for this tired Spanish traveler but, oh my, when you bring out your red laced whip! Fine women have steered me through comfortable boudoirs from Lisbon to Madrid and from London all the way to St. Petersburg. But you, my dear, you are the first to serve me the flavor of the whip. Now tell me, when might we next enjoy ourselves at both ends of your whip?"

Nancy saw to it that Carlos was regularly scheduled to join her on the third floor always within a day or to of the scheduled arrival of diplomatic pouches arriving from Madrid. Rose found the information that Nancy was reporting so compelling that she inserted herself one afternoon treating the over indulged Spaniard to a ménage–a–triose that he would still be replaying in his mind even as he lay on his death bed in Pamplona, the village of his birth, some seven years later. As he stretched himself across Nancy's lovely body while turning his bare ass toward Rose, the leather strands, first employed by one Billy Simms on the Middle Passage so many years ago, slapped across his pale skin. Soon his bum appeared as if on fire as he wiggled and winced over the bed. Only when flecks of blood soiled the silk sheets did Rose throttle back on her spirited efforts.

Three pairs of eyes exchanged quick glances as laughter exploded down the third floor hallway of Le Grand Mogul.

In 1785 Nathan Mayer Rothschild was still a boy, ten years of age, while father Mayer Amschel was traveling to the business centers of western Europe. From the father's perspective these were important years to further his financing arrangements with key clients and it was most certainly critically important that his young sons take part in certain trips. You see, Mayer Amschel never forgot his own upbringing and he understood just how impressionable youngsters are when their intellect is respected in mature settings. While it would be at least another ten years before Nathan would begin building the jewel of the Rothschild banking empire from London, he was fully alert and focused on the men his father introduced him to in Paris. Amschel, the oldest, in Frankfurt, Saloman Mayer in Vienna, Nathan to London, Carl close to the Vatican's financing powerhouse in Rome while young James would prosper in Paris – the spokes of the ship's wheel were being fashioned for a long journey years before the captain would set the first sail.

It was May of 1787. Those strolling along the Champs de Le Se enjoyed the type of pristine spring day that impressed even the Parisians. The carriage carrying father and son to their appointment with a deputy minister within the French Treasury pulled neatly to the left side of the avenue as Mayer Amschel moved quickly to step down from the cab. It was heavy on his mind that they were already ten minutes behind schedule. All taking part in the meeting would understand. The spirited horse drawing a cab across the Le Chambeau Bridge had spooked and upset a vegetable cart stationary on the corner across the boulevard. The chaos that unfolded was rather routine but enough of a problem to cause their delay. But for the senior Rothschild, any problem causing a delay was a problem to be eliminated. Time was always of the essence. Excuses were for dullards who failed to pay attention. Those reporting late to meetings were, quite simply, seen by others at the meeting in a different light. Mayer Amschel would spend as little time as possible in such shadows.

As he quickly stepped down from the carriage into the street he failed to realize that a large muddy puddle resulting from last evening's soaking shower was but a step away. Just as quickly he felt a strong left hand take hold of his right elbow. He was guided slightly away from the mud and onto the sandy gravel sidewalk. Of course, this meant that Nathan was now able to follow his father's movement away from the mess as he skipped nimbly from the carriage step onto the dry gravel. Pleased and relieved, Mayer Amschel glanced to his right to acknowledge his unseen helper. He was somewhat surprised to see that the hand belonged to a negroe. More surprising was the fact that the left hand of the man who had instinctively reached out to help was made up of a thumb and but two other fingers.

The senior Rothschild paused and tipped his cap to me. He stepped forward, looking me in the eye as he said in the French with a heavy accent that I could not recognize, "Kind sir, thanks from me to you. My apology because I hurry. Please, accept a gesture for my thanking."

My response flowed easily as I declined the two francs offered, "Merci bo que, monsieur, but most unnecessary. Good day to you and to your young companion. – Thank you, sir, but most unnecessary."

Mayer Amschel bowed slightly to me as he hurried on leading the young one by the hand. And now I must address the question that you are asking,

"Prince, will you please tell us the story as to how you reached Paris, France? " Many have called to me in this way over the years. It is because I have much to tell.

PRINCE of SAND – Chapter Thirteen – Le temps est venu de rencontrer Squire Mason / The time has come to meet Squire Mason

My years at Chicora Pines moved as quickly as any I spent in slave labor as captive to the white master. The reason, of course, was Jamie Barnwell. No period of more than ninety days would pass without Jamie arriving at the Horry plantation, or sending for me, in order to have me join him in Charleston for a month or so. Misery in the marsh is so more easily survived when you have the light of hope shining on your shoulder. In a word, this is the gift that Jamie delivered to me when my life was close to coming to a pitiful end, the gift of hope. Now understand, I owed nothing to Barnwell nor he to me. Friendship, the honest friendship that knows no debt or obligation, had surrounded us years earlier. As I have shared, I never understood why he would not make all efforts to purchase me, but I forgave him that shortcoming and my heart was free. So I was interested and surprised in the fall

of 1786 when Jamie rushed into the small brick kitchen in the corner of the yard on

Water Street where I stood happily over a slow boiling pot of grits, stirring the bubbling white concoction before adding some shrimp and crab meat,

"Prince, oh have I got news for you! Prince, please move the pot away from the flame and put down the spoon. We can warm it later. This news cannot wait!"

"Jamie, you seem concerned yet you grin like the cat standing next to the fisherman's cart at market. What is it, my friend? What is so important", I asked lightly.

"Prince, now listen, you understand that I greatly enjoy your company when you are in Charleston, correct?" Jamie was now looking at me serious.

"Yes, of course. We laugh and we sip the rum. What is this mystery?" I wanted to hear his answer.

"And you know that I would miss seeing you if you were to move away?" He asked this and I became concerned.

"Move away? Barnwell, why do you speak to me of moving away?" My brain screamed that my friend Jamie would not send me away! Oh Vordun, do not come to me out of the darkness only to snatch me away from my few moments of comfort!

"No Prince, do not worry. My story is exciting for you! Let me explain." With that comment we watered the fire and walked from the kitchen across the small lawn into the house. The perfume from the gardenia bush below my room on the second floor porch was all around me. Sitting on chairs in the drawing room, Jamie proceeded to describe a situation that I could hardly begin to believe. One of his trading partners in the colony of Virginia had told Jamie of a trip to France that a very important man in that colony, a man named Squire George Mason, was planning. This George Mason lived in a mansion like the Horry's but his mansion was smaller. The Virginia plantation was called Gunston Hall. The house stood proudly on a hill looking down to the river called Potomac. The people at Gunston Hall lived very near one of the white masters that I had heard of for many years. This man was called George Washington and his plantation home was called Mount Vernon. This grand home also looked over this Potomac River. It seemed that Mason and Washington had another friend, the man called Thomas Jefferson. The Jefferson man had been busy serving as the governor of Virginia. Jamie said that Jefferson would soon be busy again, this time going to Paris to serve the colonies of America as their Minister to France.

All of this seemed to be important to Jamie. Honestly, I could not understand why he wanted to tell this to me. And then he helped me understand. Jamie explained that Mason was now actively helping this Jefferson organize the expedition that would surround the Minister in Paris. Jamie's trading partner from Alexandria, Virginia had been more than interested when Barnwell told him of the special skills possessed by the French speaking African slave called Prince, now owned by Master Horry in the low country of South Carolina. Quickly it was determined that, should Horry agree, the group at Gunston Hall would be pleased to have me, Prince, work at Gunston Hall for a few months. If all seemed in order, it might help the office of the Minister to have a slave speaking the French to accompany the Governor Jefferson and others to Paris.

Truly excited, I leaned forward, elbows on my knees, to ask Jamie all that he knew of this Mason, this Governor Jefferson and of Paris. In the back of my brain my memory called out to me warning that such an adventure would mean, once again, climbing up into a ship of three masts with all the white men. Regarding my owner, Horry, it seemed men who owned other men found it enjoyable and sometimes to their advantage to send another man, a nigger like me, to a powerful man such as Mason or this Jefferson. Why I could not directly understand. I was bought to work the rice fields of Chicora Pines. If I am sent off to work for some other man in colony Virginia, my work cannot be given to the man who bought me in colony South Carolina. So what is the purpose for buying me in the first place?

As I was worrying on the matter of boarding another ship, Barnwell drew close to me and lowered his voice to just above a whisper. We were alone in his house, yet he turned his head from side to side, moving his eyes about as if he expected that some stranger might be in the next room trying to listen to our words. Satisfied to privacy, Jamie leaned in and told me something of Paris that rolled through me like a bolt of lightning,

"Prince, if the men at Gunston Hall feel you can truly help our group in France and you find yourself in Paris, all of your dreams of returning to being a free man could come true." Now it was my turn to focus directly on Jamie as my level of interest was large.

Jamie continued in his hushed tone,

"Prince, listen carefully. France is known as a free state and Paris a free city. If you were to walk down any street in Paris, you would do so as a 'free man'! No other man could lay claim to you, not even the old man Horry."

I do not know how I appeared to Jamie in that moment but I felt like my jaw was going to fall and slap the top of the table. Jamie had just called this city of Paris a "Free City"! Where were these free cities? How many were there? How do you get to them? Must you be invited to visit or can just anyone go and enter? The very idea that such places were out there somewhere now burned in me like our large fire in the village where we would roast the wild pigs. Oh *Vordun*, please, I beg you, show me the way to this Paris. Even if I must climb onto another three masts ship, please, *Vordun*, please show me where to go.

It was much colder than I expected when I first rode in the wagon rolling up the long tree lined drive that delivered visitors to the doorstep of Gunston Hall. Three framed windows looked down on me from the second floor of the brick home that was anchored on each side by large chimneys. Two windows faced you from either side of the large front door. Fifteen paces from the cellar pantry, which was just below the first floor on the left side of the home, was the kitchen structure where a fire was almost always kept warm. Further to the left was the small garden for spices and herbs, easily accessed just steps from the kitchen. Directly behind the home was the formal garden of English boxwoods that were arranged in an intricate pattern that was pleasant to walk through. At the far end of the garden, stretching some thirty yards from the back of the home, there was a comfortable bench where one could rest. The bench faced east, away from the house, allowing you to gaze down a gentle slope of about five hundred yards leading to the banks of the Potomac River. Like his neighbor, General Washington, who lived a few miles upriver at Mount Vernon, Squire Mason and the individuals living at Gunston Hall enjoyed easy access to the Potomac.

I cannot tell you what the rooms of Gunston Hall looked like as I never darkened that front door but I am told they are quite splendid. What I can tell you is that the cellar pantry was well appointed.

Living at Gunston Hall was something of a blur to me as so many things were happening in my life. After so many years in the shit of the 'cane with nothing new or interesting stirring in my miserable existence, suddenly it seemed that everyone I met was someone to watch and everything that happened seemed important. And so you can imagine my confusion when I met Christine Richards. Two nieces of Squire Mason were staying at Gunston Hall with their aunt and uncle when I arrived. These Richards sisters were both beautiful young ladies in Virginia, white young ladies. It was my mission to keep my head down and avoid eye contact at all cost. Jamie Barnwell had helped me understand that, for my own safety, you simply avoided certain dangers. After three or four weeks on the plantation I was summoned one Sunday morning to help with family arrangements as they prepared wagons for the short two mile ride to the church favored by the Mason family. This family was not of the catholic as I had met in Saint Domingue. These people called the church the episcopalian, a name I have always struggled to say in the English. Almost the entire day would be spent at the church as the family would visit with food and drink loaded on the wagons for the day. The neighbors of the Mason family, the General George Washington and the man called the Lord Fairfax would also bring their families and the wagons for the church day. My duty was to help load and unload the wagons and tend to the horses. No one was more shocked than me, Prince, when I went into the woods to walk one of the horses. Christine Richards followed me. I could feel her eyes on me. The farther I walked away, the closer she seemed to be to me and to the horse. I cannot explain all that happened other than to tell you that I am a man. Yes, I would have been hung from the highest tree but this Christine had her way with me. It happened and I have no more to say about that.

The governor of the Virginia colony was named Thomas Jefferson. People called it the colony of Virginia and then they would call it the state of Virginia and they spoke of a United States of America. I do not know the difference and, as you now know, I do not understand the English as well as the French. Later, in 1785, the Governor served a United States as their Minister to the French. Of course, this required him to sail on a ship of three masts to reach France. There he rode in a carriage to Paris. Minister Jefferson had been married. His wife was called Martha Skelton Jefferson and she bore him four children. On the Dahomey plain, we honor the first wife as Mother who gives us life. In our dance for Mother we cry from our knees knowing that often life is taken away from Mother because she has been in danger performing her duty to both father and son. We cry out to our Mothers who have been taken when they were giving the life to the son. The Martha who was the Jefferson wife died not long after giving the life to their daughter, Mary. When the Minister Jefferson traveled to Paris he decided to send for Mary to join him. He also decided to send for the slave, Sally Hemings, to be there with Mary. Sally Hemings was pleased because her brother, James, had already gone from their Virginia home, Monticello. He had traveled with Minister Jefferson to Paris. Sally missed her brother. Sally was fourteen years old and was pleased to go to be with Mary. Sally loved the child Mary very much. It was Sally's half-sister, the mother Martha Jefferson, who had given the life to Mary. Sally loved her niece and her heart missed her sister, Martha. I was confused but it was explained to me easily. The Martha Jefferson married to the Minister Thomas Jefferson had come to own some slaves when her father, the man called Master Skelton, had passed away. The Master Skelton was father to a slave daughter, Sally Hemings. So that is how Martha came to own her half sister, Sally, and how Sally came to live in the Paris, France.

As I have said, everything at Gunston Hall seemed to happen so fast. I was surprised and as happy as when we hunted the lion when I saw Jamie Barnwell riding in the wagon to the house at Gunston Hall. He explained to me that his Begbie and Barnwell trading house had sent him to the port called the Annapolis. Jamie traveled down to Virginia to see me and to see the Squire George Mason. Always I was so happy to see Barnwell. At this time in 1785 I was more than happy. I needed Jamie to tell me what to do. The young niece, the beautiful Christine Richards, was now living in a small house further up the river from the big house. One of my friends, a woman who worked in the kitchen, explained that this niece was with child yet she had no husband. I asked this kitchen woman, "What will she do? What will happen to this child?"

The woman shrugged and said, " Sometimes a baby is born and must be raised by all of us in the row of slave houses. It has happened before. Now a child comes again."

My face was as blank as I could manage and I said nothing. After some time passed, I asked, "So what will happen to this child?"

The woman hardly looked up. "With no father around and a mother in the big house the child will learn to live from the land. If it is a son, he will learn the work of the farm. If it is a girl, she will also work the farm and maybe she will learn the kitchen."

The woman spoke as if this had happened before which helped me fell not so much afraid. So you can see that when Jamie Barnwell was riding up the lane to Gunston Hall I was as relieved as I was happy. Jamie had sailed up for his Begbie and Barnwell trading house from Charleston to the place Annapolis. Now as he was taken inside the Gunston Hall, I realized that many big deal men came to see Squire George Mason. Later that evening I had the chance to sit down and talk with my friend, Jamie. My story about the woman Christine caused trouble to his eyes. Still, he was not mad at me. He looked out of the window for a long time and was sad when he spoke to me,

"Prince, if you are ever on the streets of Paris you will be a free man. Please. My friend, please promise me that you will not return to America because this woman is with child."

I looked at Jamie for only a moment and smiled, "Poor Jamie. Do not be sad. I will see this "free-city" they call Paris. Then I will know the way to take the trails so when I return with my son we will be free in that city!" Jamie simply shook his head and there was no more talk of such things.

Now I spoke to Jamie of my struggle to learn the English. Jamie reached into his bag and pulled out a book. "Prince," he said, "this is called a bible. It is also called the Good Book. You can practice the English with this book. Many who know the English will want to help you read this book."

Holding the book, I realized that it was large and I said to Jamie, "This book is so large and so many words I do not understand. How can I learn the English with such a book?"

"Small parts at a time, Prince. Small parts. Open the book in the middle", was Jamie's advice.

I opened the book to the place called 'palms'. Jamie told me to read the palm that is called palm ninety-one. Even today, there is much in the palm that confuses me but I love the palm ninety-one. The palm says, "Thou shalt tread upon the lion and the adder: the young lion and the dragon shalt thou trample under feet. Because he hath set his love upon me, therefore will I deliver him: I will set him on high, because he hath known my name."

Oh *Vordun*, why were we not speaking with this god of the lion when the net was dropped upon us?

PRINCE of SAND – Chapter Fourteen – Vous donner à une femme / Giving Yourself to a Woman

Going to Paris in September of 1786 was just a regular trip. As you know, this was very unusual for me. Any long journey on a three mast ship had been difficult for me but you already know this. Our group, mostly the white men traveling to join the Minister Thomas Jefferson, came to the town called Annapolis. Some of the men spoke the French.

I had already learned that the woman Christine had given birth to a daughter. I had a daughter! It was said that both the baby and her mother were well. My heart was warm and Vordun smiled on me when I became a father. The three mast ship was not such a fear as before. It was time for me, Prince, to learn the way to find the free city, the Paris. Later, when she could travel, I would return for my daughter. She would always be Sanja. As we gathered on the boards of the deck and set sail for Calais in the France I turned and faced land to the west. Silently I called to her,

"Sanja, do not worry. Your father Yamar will now go to find this place. Vordun has told me of your beauty. My heart is full of love for you, my Sanja."

Again, some of the men onboard spoke the French. It was good to speak with them as we sailed to Calais. I worked to help keep the ship in good order. I learned about their work for the Minister Jefferson. They would ask me about my left hand. By now, I had lied so often about being pushed forward while working in the sugarcane mill that it seemed to be true. We arrived in Calais where everyone spoke the French. I worked to help unload all of our trunks and crates onto the dock. It was then my job to help load many trunks onto wagons for the trip to the Paris. My excitement at being in the France was great. Everyone spoke the French quickly. It seemed to me that I now spoke so slowly but it was all good. I was able to understand almost everything.

I cannot describe Paris to you if you have never been. My work in the English allows me to have some discussion but I cannot describe for you the beauty of the City. Ooh la-la!

My age in December of 1786 was forty-two. After the first few months I was able to walk in many directions from the Ministry for a United States where Minister Jefferson worked. There were three of us slaves who lived in small rooms in the cellar of a small building near the Ministry. Other slaves, including James Heming who worked as a personal servant to Minister Jeffereson, lived in grand homes rented by the Ministers from a United States. One such junior minister, Mister Hagood Burris from Charleston, would often join me on these walks. I now spoke the French quite well. Minister Burris enjoyed being with a servant from the ministry who could communicate so well with the French.

It was a cool crisp afternoon in March, 1787 when Hagood suggested we stop by the now famous dress shop, Le Grand Mogol. The owner of the shop Mademoiselle Bertin, was a friend to Hagood. I suggested to Minister Burris,

" Hagood, I will wait outside. It is not too cold and there are always pleasant people to meet on the streets of Parris."

"Yes, Prince I shall not be long with the Madamoiselle", was Hagood's response.

Only minutes had passed when Rose Bertin stepped out from the shop followed closely by Hagood. Hagood spoke,   " Prince, the Madam and I must walk a few blocks to meet with a friend. She insists that you wait inside and enjoy the comfort of the shop until we return." I bowed from the waist after facing Rose Bertin and said, "Merci bo que, Madam."

She replied in the French " Allow me to introduce my manager, Madam Nancy Simms. She will care for you until I return."

With that said, Rose and Hagood were off and already half a block a way. I turned and stepped inside of the La Grand Mogol. The vision standing just inside the door was Nancy Simms. My breath rushed out of my lungs. Immediately I cut my eyes from hers and stared at the ground just to the right of her feet. This beautiful woman who just blinded me with her smile then spoke, "Monsuirere Prince please come inside and warm yourself."

She reached down forcing me to shake hands with my right hand and held it for an awkward moment of silence until I met her gaze. She continued, " My name is Nancy Simms. Welcome"

Now my manners and training took hold as I replied, " Madam you are too kind. I will sit here by the door and wait the return of Minister Burris. Thank you."

"Monsieur Prince our foyer area is much too busy on days such as this. Please, follow me back to one of our workshop areas where we can have a visit while you wait."

Turning on her heel she began to walk (or float) down a short hallway before entering a room off to her right. The rich oriental carpet that ran down the hallway did not turn into the dress shop work area. Of course I had no choice but to follow. In this moment I could not have told you of another name of a girl or woman. Even the name of my precious Sanja would have escaped me! Something deep within me told me that I would never leave Paris without Nancy Simms. Something deep within me told me that I would follow Nancy Simms anywhere in the world.

Now my life was moving so quickly that everything seemed to stop. The spring in Paris during 1787 was magnifique. During our first visit on that day in March it was clear that we both enjoyed speaking with one another very much. Jamie Barnwell had been my closest friend but now there was only one "best" friend and her name was Nancy Simms.

My work for the Ministry was routine and not difficult. Mostly, I raked the grounds, trimmed certain trees and shrubbery and listened to the local Parisians who worked at the Ministry. Clearly, the main reason I was part of the trip to the Ministry was my speaking the French. In private, I could give directions to our Ministers as to how to find their way around Paris. More important, I could tell them what other members of the French Ministry had to say bad about us. It was always special for me if the Parisians said bad things about us. I would try my best to remember who said what and pass that information directly to the young Minister, Hagood Burris. As I said, the work was routine and I was busy.

Nancy and I began to meet regularly. We would stroll over the boulevards and cross the River Seine. It was difficult for me to understand how men and women had actually built such beautiful things. Cathedrals, homes, statues, churches – the size and the beauty of Paris in May was beyond my mind. Nancy helped explain to me the history of Europe. She spoke of her Liverpool home in the England, the beauty of Spain and the wonders of Italy. I tried to understand but mostly I just enjoyed spending time and talking with Nancy.

We spent more and more time by sharing our stories. Nancy was fascinated to hear me describe Africa. She became familiar with my mother, Sanja, and my father, Kalem. She cried hard and long when I tried to describe the Middle Passage that took three hundred of us to Saint-Domingue. Our talks were in the French and she taught me to speak in the way of the Parisians. Nancy was thrilled when I told her of meeting the youngster, Alexander Hamilton, who introduced me to Jamie Barnwell in Christiansted, St. Croix. Her tears of pain changed to tears of joy when I shared with her my arrival and visits to Charleston. Nancy would hold my hands in hers and speak of her hope to someday visit Charleston with me.

Rarely did we speak of her story and the port of Liverpool in the England. Any talk of her family made her sad. She did love the beauty of the River Mersey and would tell me about some happy visits to the river. She had last seen the England while staring from a three masted ship looking at the cliffs in a place called Dover. She said that the cliffs were white, white like chalk. I told her that I hoped to see these cliffs someday. I asked Nancy why her memories of Liverpool made her so sad. Nancy simply shrugged and mentioned that her mother had to work so long and hard in a tavern while her father was always away on a three masted ship. She would smile and speak of meeting the Mademoiselle Rose Bertin while standing on the Liverpool docks.

In Paris, Nancy lived in three rooms in a house that was close to Le Grand Mogol. I will never forget that day, Saturday, May 12, 1787. Nancy was filled with excitement, more than usual. After a short stroll in a park near the shop, Nancy leaned toward me to whisper in my ear,

"Prince, can we please walk to my house? I have a surprise to share with you!"

Her eyes sparkled as I made my bow and, taking her hand in mine, made a flourish regarding the beautiful Mademoiselle and my pledge to obey her every command. When we reached her house I immediately saw that the fine table in the kitchen was already covered with plates of breads, meats and cheese that she had earlier made ready. Nancy had arranged her rooms with the bedroom on the window looking down on Richelieu Boulevard. Her comfortable sitting room / library and the kitchen /dining area were well kept with fine furniture. She poured wine for us. It was 4:00 in the afternoon and I would not need to return to my room at the Ministry until 10:00 that night. After enjoying the delightful offerings and after almost an hour had passed, Nancy reached across the table and took my mangled left hand in both of hers. She looked directly into my eyes as she held my hand to her cheek. She kissed my hand gently, many times, never taking her eyes from mine. She walked me from the dining area leading me into her bedroom. Now she turned to me and placed her hands on my shoulders. Nancy then said,

"Prince, I have a favor to ask."

"Anything, my Nancy", came my reply.

"Please, I beg you, please make love to me and stay with me tonight for as long as you can."

The peace and excitement of being desired in this way by a beautiful young woman who I treasured as my friend was an evening that I can never forget. Living in misery and suffering loss every day as a slave shatters the spirit. The body and the soul can only mend and heal but so much under such stress. You cannot be healed until you know for certain just what is missing. Love touched me in so many ways just as this same love had left me a stranger when I was shoved below deck on the *Nelly*. Honest affection from one who is held in respect can cut out hatred that has been hurled upon you by hundreds, or so it seemed to me. In this bedroom on this night I was a complete man. Different from the youngster who had struck out to hunt wild pigs on the Dahomey plain but similar in that all that I held dear was surrounding me in Nancy's room. Slowly we helped each other out of our clothes. There was no shame or hesitation but I was full of wonder and craved to see all of Nancy in her full beauty. All of my senses were alert with my sense of touch being particularly aroused. Nancy placed her hands on me as she wished and encouraged me to treat her the same. Small gasps from each of us escaped when a particular pinch or rub felt so amazing. I did not cry yet I felt strong emotions that often might lead to tears. We were both happy and curious at the same time. Quickly we became more familiar and free with sharing our bodies. You will understand that I never wanted this moment to end. Even today, I think of those first moments of exploring each other with full acceptance and permission from both. We were two but we were becoming one. Oddly, I recall thinking how pleased I was that I had not hung myself in Saint Domingue and felt myself clever to have only lost two fingers from my left hand in the trade.

As happens with lovers who have waited many days to answer the call from their loins, Nancy and I quickly took each other freely in physical expressions of such mutual attraction. Time became meaningless as long stretches of being together were measured by degrees of satisfaction in ways that made the hands of the clock nearly invisible. Long drinks of cool water and rubbing one another with dry towels were acceptable pauses to the unfolding passion that was given a free rein. Finally, stretched across the bed in states of exhausted bliss, Nancy rose and walked casually from the bed into her sitting room. I listened as she moved something from the floor and heard her call to me;

"Prince, lay out on your stomach and do not peek. I order you to obey my commands", she ordered. I relaxed on the bed.

PRINCE of SAND – Chapter Fifteen - Secrets
d'apprentissage / Learing Secrets

Ten years would pass before I could understand just what Nancy, Rose Bertin, Hagood Burris, Senior Carlos Montague, Alexander Hamilton, Mayer Amschel Rothschild and others were involved in when they gathered information and passed along their secrets. Some of the information was traded or sold in order to position soldiers or sailors to fight against an enemy. Other secrets would be shared in efforts to put large amounts of money to make what they called, "the investments." My roll, the roll of the Prince, would be small but I would not hesitate to do anything that Nancy would ask of me.

During that summer of 1787, I began to learn about different countries—of England, Germany, Spain, Italy and the rumors from Belgium. Hagood Burris, working in the Ministry of a United States, advised Nancy that the experts in Belgium warned that King Louis and his queen, Marie Antoinette, were in much danger. The same breeze of freedom that blew across a United States was pushing revolution within certain countries within the Europe. Just as the blind eye of the cuckold is the last to see, so too the royal couple in Versailles did not see danger.

I must tell you, Nancy and I had become more than lovers, enjoying the romance that is the Paris spring. We were soul-mates, brother and sister in many ways, as we learned what we shared.

You know that on Saturday, May 12 we lay together for the first time across Nancy's bed. It was now the 16th day of May in the early evening. I was not required to return to my room at the Ministry until midnight.

As lovers often do, we now moved more quickly through the 'normal' joys of coupling. Even at my age of 43, in May of 1787, I was still very young. In the ways of amour, my Nancy, at the tender age of 26, was my teacher. Every good man should have the blessing of such a young lover.

It was between 8:00 and 9:00, as I remember, when my Nancy laughed her naughty giggle. After I looked to her, I saw that she had stepped into her sitting room. I called to her playfully, "Little Bird. Little Bird of the Love, stop hiding from your warrior who stalks the mighty Lion. Return to your bed and love me. I demand this of you now."

She laughed again and gave me an order of her own. "You may become scared or you may become scarred, but you will do as General Nancy commands!" Turn your head from this door, lay flat on the bed. You may not turn until I permit it. DO YOU UNDERSTAND?"

"Oh yes, my General of Love. Please teach me how I must behave!", came my response.

I could hear Nancy standing next to my buttocks as she opened some kind of box and dropped it to the floor.

"Take that you beast." She laughed as she softly drew a soft whip across my back.

Returning her laughter, I roared, "Dare you call that a whipping my love bitch? Harder now so that I know you are there."

Now she whipped me carefully as I turned to take her in my arms. Immediately and easily, I reached up and took from her the small hand whip. Such a whip is often referred to as a "cat-a-nine tails." I flicked once and then again against here lily white ass. She giggled with delight.

And then I froze. No man could move me. Nancy called out, "Why did you stop?"

From the bottom that is within me rose a roar, "The *NELLY* !?!"

I dropped to my knees. All I could do is stare at the red-laced handle closed within my three fingers as I continued to mumble, "*Nelly...Nelly...Nelly.*"

Nancy now ran to her door to assure a neighbor that all was well. She had explained that I had awakened from a bad dream.

Billy Simms! Oh Vordun, what wicked man could follow me so? I could not look at my Nancy yet I needed so to know.

What? When? Where? Is this Billy Simms prowling Paris? I must stalk him like the dog that he his and kill him tonight! With my hands I will kill him. As a warrior of the Yorabun, he will stand no chance. Still, I must stalk him. I must kill him. And feed his balls to the fish this very night!

Cold towels? Water. Cold water and a pan. Bathed with cold towels? I see no blood. This is good? No blood! Cold towels on my neck. Cold towels placed on my eyes and the sides of the head. And then I can hear her. Faintly at first, as if she's outside the window but no, she is not outside. Nancy is beside me and now I can hear her voice clearly; "Prince, Prince. Yamar, my Yamar. Love is around my Prince. Only love. Look at me Yamar."

Firmly now, "Look at me Prince."

Our eyes were together, quietly she spoke, "Yes my father sailed on the *Nelly* and I never saw anyone on that ship but crew."

I jumped without thinking as if Vordun had thrown the lightening from a cloud. I jumped.

Nancy threw her arms around me and whispered, "Dead. Dead. Dead and gone. Many years have gone. I was 10 years old. Dead. Billy Simms is dead."

Still stunned, I pulled away.

With my hands on her shoulders I stared into her face. "How?" I asked.

"What Yamar?"

She could not hear me.

"How did Billy Simms die?", I asked.

There was a long pause. Nancy looked up at me. "Shit." She said.

"I do not understand." Was my response.

"My father was sick on the *Nelly* and he shit himself to death."

Falling back on the bed I almost died—from the laughing.

PRINCE of SAND – Chapter Sixteen - Du rire et des larmes .. Move! /From the Laughter and the Tears .. Move!

Whatever conversations came next with my Nancy, it was that and more. But, as I have told you, we shared our stories in many ways. Now Billy Simms was put into place. I will tell you, however, that I always felt a sadness for her mother, the good woman Janet.

It was in this year of 1787 that Nancy made yet another new friend at Le Grand Mogol. Years earlier the Minister Jefferson from a United States had introduced his slave, James Hemings, to Mademoiselle Bertin. Late in the year of 1787, it was October I believe, Minister Jefferson paid a visit accompanied by James' younger sister, Sally Hemings.

Just as I had first met Nancy as Rose conducted business with Minister Hagood Burris, now Nancy spent time visiting with young Sally as Minister Jefferson visited with Rose on the third floor of Le Grand Mogol.

This was rare as only "unofficial" business and/or the trading of secrets ever seemed to take place on that floor. Nancy told me that the Hemings girl, Sally, was 14 years old but to me, she looked more like 12.

Nancy and Sally became close friends. My Nancy had that way with good people. I only met Sally briefly over the next two years and by 1779 many people were on the move. Something called the "French Revolution" was getting ready to start. There was a doctor in Paris by the name of Dr. Guillotine who they said made quite a contribution. The King lost his head in this revolution! Everything seem to turn upside down. Nancy had a long talk with her young friend, Sally. Nancy said, "Sally, you must speak to me about the Minister Jefferson. Is he good to you?"

Sally looked down and spoke quietly, "I will not speak about the Minister to you."

"Sally, you must! You are in Paris and Paris is a free city. Has anyone spoke to you about such things?" asked Nancy.

Sally raised her eyes, "Yes, my brother James has told me about the Free City."

Nancy continued, "And the Minister Jefferson, has he told you about the Free City?"

"Yes, Nancy, the Minister and I have talked about such things," responded Sally.

Nancy took Sally by her hands and spoke, "Sally, listen to me very carefully. I can help you be safe staying here in Paris, here in the Free City. Please, Sally, please will you stay?"

Sally looked up and squeezed Nancy's hands. As she spoke a single tear rolled over her right cheek. "No."

I left Paris first. Nancy followed a few weeks later with the members of the delegation of a United States. We landed at the place Annapolis in the Maryland colony. It was late in 1790 that Nancy and I learned that the slaves of Saint-Domingue had stood up. We were told that these slaves removed the hands of the slave-masters who had worked so long to hold them down in Saint-Domingue. Now we understood that many French men, women and children were put to their deaths by the new free people from Africa in this place. We have talked that, in the worship of Vordun, the blood of the chicken is collected in a bowl of sacrifice. I have been told that the catholic will put wine in a cup and call it blood from their jesus. The first to drink of the blood in the worship of Vordun is the high Priest or Priestess. They tell me that the people in the catholic stand in line for the blood of the jesus. I stopped and I prayed to Vordun, "Oh Vordun, let those men and women in Saint-Domingue, now free, who have earned it—let them be allowed to first taste the blood."

It was time for movement. I had returned to Gunston Hall but now my only visits to the fields were to help bring the children to the small schoolhouse that sat just to the right of the Hall. Nancy spent time visiting up in the city called Philadelphia. Many plans were being made for a new city very near Gunston Hall that would be called the

Washington for the grand general up the river at Mt. Vernon. But for me, amazing work took place in the schoolhouse. You see, my little Sonja was sometimes brought to the schoolhouse. Nobody but me thought of her as Sonja and they all called her Janet. But she was my Sonja and I would watch her walk from the kitchen building across the front of Gunston Hall over to the schoolhouse. My heart floated when she walked or skipped to her lessons.

Once again, my joy was greatly increased when my friend, Jamie Barnwell, made a trip up from Charleston. As the years were moving on and I was almost 50 years old, I would not return to Charleston with Jamie. He seemed excited to tell me that old Mr. Middleton at Chicora Pines no longer owned me but now Squire Mason here at Gunston Hall was my new owner. Honestly, it did not seem much difference to me. Once I had been to Paris and moved some secrets with Nancy, I was treated more like a human being. It seemed to make some of these people happy.

One thing I can tell you that was very exciting to me and to my Nancy was what had happed to my young friend, the Alexander Hamilton. Do you now remember how I told you of the boy in the trading house of Christiansted in St. Croix? The youngster who had arranged my trade from my friend Nicolas Dumas to my friend Jamie? Well, you must listen to this! The Alexander Hamilton came to America to the New York! He became close with the great George Washington. Jamie and Nancy both told me secrets about how Hamilton, now a great man of a United States of America, helped to build the First Bank of a United States. Nancy was very excited to tell me that her friend, Mayer Amschel Rothschild, had helped the young Hamilton get this Bank in operation. My Nancy liked very much for me and Jamie to tell her our story of meeting Hamilton in Christiansted.

Once Nancy took me with her on a smaller boat up to the town of Philadelphia. We were to meet some men on the docks to trade some secrets. It surprised me when a carriage stopped and the Secretary Hamilton stepped out. I did not think about it twice. I simply looked at him and said, "Good morning young Master Hamilton. We met many years ago in Christiansted."

As the fine Hamilton turned to face me, I placed my left hand on top of a whiskey keg in front of me. Raising his eyes from my three fingers, Hamilton stepped toward me. Placing his hands on my shoulders, he asked speaking the French, "Merci. Please, my good friend, how are you and where have you come to live?"

It was wonderful to see him again and obviously doing so well. Quickly in the French I replied, "Minister Hamilton, the trade you arranged through Monsieur Barnwell has served me well leading me to Charleston, Annapolis, Paris and now I live at Gunston Hall with Squire Mason, close to your General Washington. By the way, your French has only improved, your Eminence, and I congratulate you fully.

Now, if it pleases you, may I present my friend and partner in all things from Paris, the distinguished Mademoiselle Nancy Simms, who for years assisted the distinguished Rose Bertin in operating the finest Parisian salon, La Grand Mogol. These ladies dressed the poor victim, Queen Marie Antoinette, and her ladies in waiting over many years before the Revolution. Your Excellency, Monsieur Hamilton, I present Mademoiselle Nancy Simms."

If thunder always followed lightening, the clap of the thunder would have rolled over Philadelphia that morning. Even the well-spoken Hamilton was struck by the beauty of the Mademoiselle. Hamilton stared at Nancy, cut me a quick look in amazement and returned his eyes to feast on Miss Simms. "Mademoiselle, please consider me at your service and please forgive my poor manners in failing to anticipate the visit of such an artist as a designer from Le Grand Mogol. Philadelphia is open to your charm."

"The honor is mine, Secretary Hamilton and may I add my voice to so many, particularly my friends from the Rothschild family in Frankfort, who so beautifully sing your praise," was my Nancy's gracious reply.

It seemed to me that Hamilton shifted from one foot to another when Nancy mentioned her friend, the Jew called Mayer Amschel Rothschild, but perhaps I did not see that correctly.

As swiftly as could be accomplished in comfort, Nancy accepted Secretary Hamilton's invitation to join him in his carriage and they were off to see parts of Philadelphia where the secrets are shared. The rest of my day was spent comfortably on board our ship where masts no longer held such fear for me as in my younger days.

The movement from the city back to the new town of Washington or Alexandria, close to Gunston Hall, would take place from time to time when Nancy asked me to help her with a secret. My heart was broken when the woman, Christine, decided to go to Philadelphia to live and my beautiful Sonja joined her there. But I had never been allowed to truly join my daughter. The owner of a slave would be so cruel as to control who could live like a father and who had to stay a stranger. But my heart still loves my Sonja, always.

Nancy had told me of big movement back in France and in the year 1799, when I was then fifty-five years old and Nancy thirty-eight. We learned that the French General Napoleon Bonaparte had seized the power of the France. Over the next four years, the movement was big and it was fast. It was in 1800 that the Spain made a secret trade to give the France all of what was called the Louisiana so Spain would take over a kingdom in the Italy called Etruria. My Nancy helped move some of these secrets. In 1803, the Napoleon sent many troops to the New Orleans port and the President of a United State, now the Minister Thomas Jefferson, sent many secrets using Nancy. Some said Napoleon would tell his soldiers to sail to Port-Au-Prince. Others said no, but then the England said they would do another war against the France. The Napoleon sold off all the Louisiana to President Jefferson and a United States became very much bigger. Nancy was always in movement when these secrets were shared and I helped when I could. We liked the New Orleans where the French was spoken well.

While these movements were taking place in America, the young Nathan Mayer Rothschild followed the plan designed by his father. Nathan was twenty-one years old in 1798 when he moved to Manchester, England first working as a trader in textiles. By the time he was twenty-nine, in 1806, he was a banker married to the Hanna Cohen and the Rothschild empire was underway. Nancy explained to me that these children of Meyer Amschel Rothschild were growing up to be the bankers of the world. It was still confusing to me but I understand that their movement of the money was big and it was fast.

Nancy visited her friend, Sally Hemings, from time to time. Sally now lived in the White House, the name for the President's large house, if she was not in Monticello. I believe that for both it was chance to remember Paris and to speak the French. One night, after a long visit, Nancy came to the house where we stayed and we talked a long time. Sally had been sad. She told Nancy about a dream of her sister, Martha, that was coming back night after night. It was Martha who was married to the Thomas Jefferson when she died. Sally was so sad that her sister Martha was dead. Everyday she walked to where Martha was buried wearing a white dress. The dress was heavy and dragged along the ground because the dress was soaked with Sally's tears. Everyday, Sally walked to the burial site in the white dress soaked with the tears. Finally, in the dream, the Thomas Jefferson told Sally that she must top soaking the dress in tears or she will ruin the dress dragging it on the ground.

After listening, my Nancy put her arms around young Sally. She told her not to be so sad but to be happy about her dream.

Sally asked her, "But how can I be happy? The white dress is soaked with my tears every night."

Nancy explained, "Oh, my little kitten your sister Martha loves you very much. It is your sister who tells you to stop crying. You have almost washed away the white dress with your tears. The time has come to stop and to be happy in your dress. Your sister loves you."

Sally smiled and put her own arms around the lovely Nancy.

This year, this year of 1804 as I had turned sixty years old seemed to be going so well. It was going so well until the bastard, the one they called Aaron Burr, turned like a snake on July 11th and shot our beloved Hamilton dead.

PRINCE of SAND – Chapter Seventeen - o Vordun, Aidez-nous à couper le serpent / O Vordun, Help Us to Cut the Snake

What can I tell you? I am a man, a man much older than the boy who trembled on his knees at the site of the three mast ship. My good friend, Jamie Barnwell, had treated me like a human being. Jamie was so excited he almost cried when he told me my speaking the French could carry me to a Free City they called Paris. I was pulled into the salon in Paris to meet an angel called Nancy and the Prince was loved. I love this woman and she is my friend. One young man, the boy Alexander Hamilton, he wanted to speak with me in Christiansted. He wanted to speak to me!

The white man crushed me whenever it suited him. The powerful black men who sold me to the white man had large bags of gold coins. But Hamilton sensed that the Creole, Nicolas Dumas, wanted to sell while Barnwell wanted to buy. Now they told us that the asshole called Burr was alive and Hamilton was dead. Dead? But Burr was captured and certainly he would hang. Yet he went free and we learned he was in the London, England! How this happened I cannot say but Nancy and I were both sad.

Years passed and the grey skies were not so sad. Life was good to both of us. Nancy had secrets to move. Her friend, Rose Bertin, had been able to keep Le Grand Mogol and Nancy actually was in Paris for almost a year. I was strong for a man at sixty. The sugarcane had almost killed a young Prince but the older Prince had good food to eat and a warm bed to sleep in. Vordun blessed me and I drank the blood of the chicken, which kept my eyes sharp and my hearing as alert as the lion. I was ready to hunt if my stomach was empty.

Nancy had returned form the France and it was 1811 with me moving well at sixty-seven years old when the important secret reached Nancy. She did not look like a woman of fifty years but more like forty years old and her eyes sparkled at the news.

The snake was coming back across the ocean. England had sent him away so Burr had crawled into France. With no prospects, our secret trader learned that the man who took our Hamilton's life would come back into a United States at New York. I have seen my Nancy excited and I have seen her trade the secrets but never have I seen her plan and spring such a trap.

"Move the money," Nancy mumbled. "The asshole will think he can move the big money."

"What?" I asked her. "I cannot understand."

"Nothing, my Prince. I am just thinking even in his failure, this man Burr believes that he is too clever to remain out of the money. It will be well. We must get him to believe he is moving where he wants to go."

The planning began in a serious way as the arrival of Burr from the France was scheduled. As was often the case in working the secrets, my role would not be so big but the job would be important. The man who helped trade the secrets agreed to work with us and his role would be very important.

Nancy went over our plan and we talked about it in many ways.

"Prince, his ship is expected into the harbor on April 12th. Please, go over the plan again."

"His arrival is April 12th and we will have eyes on him as they unload. We will not assume where in New York he will stay or assume he stays in New York. It will be important to see who visits him. We must visit him before he leaves New York," came my reply.

"Yes," commented Nancy. "And what will come next?"

"You can explain to our secret trader that you must meet him. It can be at his house but perhaps it is best at a tavern or public house where food and drink are served when the lights will be low. Now, Nancy, tell me what you will say," was my practiced response.

"Prince, when our trader introduces me I will pull back the hood of my cape and smile at him as if on the Champs de le Sey. I will say, "Mr. Vice President, welcome back to your home and thank you for all you have done for America. My name is Mrs. Morgan Van Landingham and I have lived in Newport, Rhode Island since the death of my husband, Paul, eight years ago. It was my husband's dream and passion to help dismantle the grotesque central bank erected by the bastard, Hamilton, and return the movement of capital through the state banks as originally chartered. Please, Mr. Vice President, please help me to move the capital that my husband and others have accumulated."

Our secret trader told us that Burr might be living on the ship. "Prince, we must get his attention and put our practiced routine into actioin. Tell me what we will take upon the ship?" asked Nancy.

"We will move onto the ship in the evening when it is dark. Burr will need to already be on the ship. I will carry two jugs of rum and be up on the deck above the captain's quarters. Nancy, how will you proceed to the captain's quarters?" was my question back to my friend.

"Prince, I will proceed directly to the captain's quarters with the stated goal to conduct and complete private business. I will carry my bag with a change of clothes, my perfumed dressing gown, the leather pouch with two small stones and the small sharp knife. The two items we have discussed will be tied around my shoulders under my cape." Quickly now we covered our plan—again and again the details were discussed. In the evenings, we rowed out to a sloop where we practiced the movements of our plan. The ship carrying the traitor Burr would be in New York harbor soon.

The energy for our goals was very high but sometime you can practice too much. I wanted to see this man, Burr. I wanted to work the plan.

And then our trader of the secrets was in the house with us. The three mast ship from France had anchored about midway out in the harbor. Our trader gave a report,

"Our plan will change. We know where he went the first night and our people watched that house, but Burr returned to the ship the next day. The plan will change because he lives on the ship. We have planned to find him in the house but he lives on the ship. We need to know where on the ship he is living." The secret trader did not seem upset but this was his report.

Nancy spoke, "We will practice the plan as if he lives in the captain's quarters and get direct intelligence before the meeting. Given our plans for departure, it is possible that this living on the ship is a good thing." As always, Nancy thought clearly and spoke wisely.

Quickly now the meeting was set. Our secret trader got word to Burr that the distinguished Mrs. Van Landingham from Newport was anxious to meet him that very evening. This would mean that Burr's attendants would have no time to ask around New York about the Van Landingham's in Newport. It was suggested that the two first meet in the McSorley Public House only two blocks off of the harbor near the ship holding Burr.

It was not my job to be at this meeting but I know that Nancy entered the tavern fully covered by her hood. Once seated with Burr, she revealed her gorgeous hair, presented in the latest fashion, while displaying a bosom that would not normally be seen in Manhattan before 10:00 p.m. Burr was totally moved and wanted only for their evening visit on board the ship to arrive. Nancy was most convincing in explaining to Monsieur Burr that he, and he alone, could turn the financial levers needed to stall the out-of-control national bank. Burr was fully intoxicated at the idea that New York wanted and needed him in power before he even set foot on the dock!

The evening was set. Our people could confirm—Burr lived in the captain's quarters. Nancy and I stepped into the rowboat in which two sailors manned the oars. The beautiful evening was marked by a calm sea and our trip to the ship was short and easy. I scampered up the netting and lowered steps quickly and turned to help Nancy. As I had planned, no one needed to be in touch with Nancy as I helped her onto the deck. She avoided eye contact with a sailor as I directed her to the captain's quarters without ever asking permission from anyone. You can be sure that Burr was more than happy to see Mrs. Van Landingham wanting to enter his quarters. Nancy glanced at me with a small smile as I announced her and she took Burr's welcoming older hand. She turned her back to me and I held her cloak tightly at the shoulders. She slipped out of the wrap, which I folded in the manner we had practiced as Burr led her to a table full of wine and meats.

Now the trap was being set and I quickly moved back up the steps to the deck were I had placed my two jugs of rum. Only two sailors were left on board as others enjoyed liberty. The two watched me unload. They were peering down the steps to look toward the lady in Burr's quarters. Talking fast I pushed the larger jug into their greedy hands. I suggested that they move forward to the fore deck and keep watch as I would stand on the steps of aft deck. Laughing, I told them this 8:00 p.m. watch would certainly not be over before 10:00 p.m. The jug of rum and the idea of being left alone pleased them greatly.

Two hours can be a long time to wait when you are preparing for a long journey. I thought of them all—my Nancy and the best of friends, Jamie Barnwell. My mother, Sonja, and my own Sonja. But so often my mind returned to Hamilton and Vordun. Oh Vordun, if only you could replace the serpent Burr with the fine Hamilton and leave this rotten ship of snakes to sink on her anchor!

But it was getting near the time and it was important to execute every step of the plan exactly right. By now I had made sure the second jug was also in the hands of the sailors and the they would not become barriers to us in reaching our goal. As the clock read 10:00 p.m., I was moving down the stairs when the first shot rang out. As I had removed Nancy's cloak, I had made sure to grab the cord that was hanging around her shoulders. Two pistols had been primed and made ready to fire as they were tied to each end of the cord. The red handle pistol carried a ball as well as powder. The black handle pistol was prepared in the the same manner as when used by Jamie Barnwell and Charlton Morrison as Francis and Cheshire Owen had screamed in the sitting room all those many years ago—all powder and no ball.

Calmly now, Nancy stepped out of the captain's quarters handing me the red handle pistol with smoke still drifting from the barrel. As I slipped the fired weapon in the leather case under my garment, Nancy stood facing the closed door to the captain's quarters with the black handle pistol in one hand and a red handled cat-o-nine tails in the other. Just as dancers might enter the stage, the two wide eyed sailors, drunk with rum and frightened from the shot, stumbled halfway down the steps where I helped them back with a laughing welcome.

"Watch out lads, the ladies are roaring tonight!"

Now Nancy, naked except for her slippers, fired the black handle pistol into the air doing no harm but making noise and smoke! Throwing her head back, she roared in laughter, "Shoot at me, will you, you salty dog! Get ready for the whip!"

The exotic Nancy moved back into the room with all views into the captain's quarters blocked by doors, smoke and cloaks. I clasped the two drunks by their shoulders and moved them all the way up the steps and over to the main mast. It was there that our secret trader stepped out of the shadows and dropped a belaying pin onto the backs of their heads. These men would sleep well into the next day.

Within minutes Nancy climbed the steps onto the deck in her fully professional manner. Any trace of her presence below decks was gone other than Burr lying in a bed with cord bound around his mouth. His testicles were no longer attached. They were nesting in a small leather pouch carried by Nancy and weighted with two stones. The two rum jugs I had carried aboard were sent into the sea. Our job was completed and now our practiced departure unfolded.

Nancy stepped into a small boat and was rowed to a dock where she was assisted into a waiting carriage whose next planned stop was a destination that had not been shared with us. My boat rowed me out into the harbor to a ship bound for a location that had not been revealed to us. I very much hoped that Port-Au-Prince was the port of call. Pistols and the leather pouch were slipped over the side with rocks weighting them down never to be found. Only the secret tracker was left standing on the dock. Without looking back, I heard him quietly call out,

"Prince, please tell us one of your stories for you have been many places and seen many things!"

In the same quiet voice I answered, "Yes, my Jamie, sometime in the years ahead, we will go to our place together and share our stories. You are my friend in all ways … always."

~ ~ ~

The author completed Prince of Sand on Thursday, October 26, 2017 working in Hopeway George C. Covington Library in Charlotte, NC.

Made in the USA
Columbia, SC
21 February 2018